Praise for *Time for Me*

"Ruth has struck gold once again. Her newest book, *Time for Me*, reads like a gentle invitation to both old readers and new ones alike to grab hold of the idea that change—any change that would be beneficial to make—is always possible. She lays out the process for making the change in a clear, simple way. Nothing is too hard when taken in small bites, a week at a time. This book is sure to be a winner among those folks who have not given up on the idea that we are never too old to change."

—**Karen Casey,** author of *Each Day a New Beginning*
and *Living Long, Living Passionately*

"Ruth has worked for many years to feed the souls and spirits of all her clients and contacts. Her depth of caring is evident in her books and through her workshops and events. Some authors write a book or two. Ruth's commitment and passion is a lifelong endeavor that has enriched the lives of many. Follow her work and feel the healing happen."

—**Sharon Wegscheider-Cruse,** author of
Becoming a Sage, founder of Onsite Workshops

"The book *Time for Me* offers a great plan for anyone seeking more peace and joy in their lives. Ruth Fishel writes with clarity so that the principles she explains are easily understood. Her concise and lively writing is positive and uplifting!"

—**Anda Peterson,** author of
Walks with Yogi: The Enlightenment Experiment

12-10-15
To Kelly —

Time for Me

Daily Practice for a Joyful, Peaceful, Purposeful Life

For Gentler
Time for you!
with Love +
Peace -

RUTH FISHEL

Illustrations by Bonny Van de Kamp

Ruth

Health Communications, Inc.
Deerfield Beach, Florida

www.hcibooks.com

**Library of Congress Cataloging-in-Publication Data
is available through the Library of Congress**

© 2016 Ruth Fishel

ISBN-13: 978-07573-1886-3 (Paperback)
ISBN-10: 07573-1886-X (Paperback)
ISBN-13: 978-07573-1887-0 (ePub)
ISBN-10: 07573-1887-8 (ePub)

Publisher: Health Communications, Inc.
      3201 S.W. 15th Street
      Deerfield Beach, FL 33442–8190

Illustrations © Bonny Van de Kamp
Cover and interior design by Lawna Patterson Oldfield

This book is dedicated to these wonderful people you are no longer with us:

Bill Menza

A dear friend, meditation teacher,
and wise mentor who was the epitome of a
true bodhisattva, a person who dedicates their
life to help others heal from suffering.

Jane Drury

Also a dear friend and wise sponsor,
a woman who dedicated her life to help others.

Barbara Thomas

Another dear friend who dedicated
her life to help others.

Kurt Bierig

My son-in-law, a very dear man
who was much too young to leave us and
who will be missed by many.

I am most fortunate to have known you all and to
have learned so much from you. You live through these
pages and in my heart.

Contents

With Gratitude

I am deeply grateful, as always, to my partner Sandy Bierig for her copious editing, love, and support;

To my daughters Debbie Fishel Boisseau and Judy Fishel for always being there for me;

Bonny Van de Kamp, for "getting" my thoughts in seconds and transferring them to page after page, book after book, with her wonderful artwork;

To my editor Christine Belleris, always a joy to work with, always with great patience and wonderful suggestions;

To the staff at HCI who have been so helpful with all my books;

To Lawna Oldfield for her creative skills and for capturing the essence of this book with her art for the cover and layout;

To Kim Weiss, HCI's terrific publicist, for all her enthusiasm and ideas for promoting *Time for Me*.

For Trish Fritz for finding a way to use her camera so I would look younger on the back cover!

To the following people who were so supportive, some who contributed an idea, a paragraph, some suggestions or editing, who have simply been there along the way: Richard Brady, Sharon Wegscheider-Cruse, Joann Malone, Michele Marshall, Lee Purser, Shirley Smith, Alex Lerner, MD, Viviann Plenge, Patrick Smith, Robbie Tisch, and Marilyn Warlick;

To my wonderful teachers Thich Nhat Hanh, Fred Eppsteiner, and Joanne Friday. And Bill Menza, whose spirit lives in this book;

And for Dr. Bob and Bill Wilson. Without them I would not be alive.

Introduction

How many times have you read a book and as you are reading it, know that it is life-changing? Sometimes you find new information, or a repeat of something you have already read, but you know this time, if you just practice what it suggests, your life will be better. You are so excited you tell friends to be sure to read this book! Soon, although you are well meaning, you forget. You forget to meditate in the morning. You forget that three breaths can calm you down. You forget to exercise. You forget you are powerless over many things. You forget to slow down to take time in nature. You forget the many lessons you learned in the book. And you go on to read another book. Now you say, "This is it! I can really be happy now!"

Time for Me contains wisdom proven to be true, wisdom that works if you work it, wisdom that has been true over many thousands of years. It is said that there is nothing new under the sun. This really isn't true. Science is discovering new truths all the time. One of these discoveries just happened within the past forty or fifty years. It is the field of *neuroplasticity* or brain plasticity. It found that our brains are not hardwired, as it has been thought until very recently. Scientists have now proven that we have the ability to rewire and create new neural circuits at any age! The other part of this exciting news is that *our thoughts can rewire our brain*. While it was concluded that our brains couldn't change after we were in our thirties, we now know that our brains are like plastic and can continue to change over our lifetime. For example, the more we practice something new, new neurons fire together forming new neural pathways in our brains, deepening with each repetition. So if we were to practice all this week, saying to ourself "I am happy," or "This is a happy moment," or "This is a peaceful moment," or "This is a calm moment," etc., we would be more apt to return to this thought during moments when we are feeling otherwise. In time, these pathways become deeper than the pathways made by the old habits that we are no longer practicing, therefore becoming more automatic.

Actually, the Buddha knew this 2,600 years ago. He simply didn't have the scientific proof. He discovered that our thoughts create our feelings. And he taught that if we change our thoughts we change how we feel. He didn't have scans and other modern equipment that could examine our brains to prove it. But he lived this truth and taught it and those who listened and practiced it displayed additional proof that this was true.

This is why *Time for Me* is set up for us to practice every day, one subject, one week at a time. We practice each week to create new habits that will last us a lifetime! Buddhist monk, worldwide meditation teacher and author of more than fifty books Thich Nhat Hanh teaches about changing our habits in a very easy to understand way. He explains that within us are all the "seeds" of all the characteristics that people have. He suggests we imagine that they are all stored in our basement. He calls the seeds that cause our suffering, such as anger, jealousy, and fear, the "weeds," while the characteristics that create joy in our lives such as compassion, generosity, and love, are the "flowers." The ones that grow are the ones that we water and they come up into our living room. It's up to us which ones grow.

Time for Me is a personal practice book. It is *not* a work-book. It is laid out in a weekly form to be practiced daily. It is personal because if you accomplish the simple truths found in each section in less than a week, then you simply move on. If it takes you longer, you simply practice that particular lesson for as long as it takes.

There is no right or wrong, good or bad. It just is. And as a twelve-step recovery slogan says: "It works if you work it. So work it 'cause you're worth it!"

A Very Simple Three-Step Method

❶ We Practice Mindfulness

Only by being aware of our thoughts can we change them.

❷ We Connect with Universal Energy

You can call this God, spiritual energy, Higher Power, Buddha energy, Allah, whatever you choose to call a power greater than yourself to which you feel connected.

❸ We Use the Power of Our Thoughts

Based on our new scientific understanding of neuroplasticity, we have the power to change our thoughts.

How to Make This Book Work Best for You

My original intention for *Time for Me* was that this would be a fifty-two week practice book, where you would practice one week at a time in the order it was written. As I went along writing it, it occurred to me that you, the reader, might not have a need to spend a week on the particular subject that comes up next. For example, you might not think you have anyone to forgive, or have the need to grieve. Therefore you can skip those weeks, and replace them with a practice that interests you from weeks fifty-three through fifty-eight and move on. On the other hand, you might have a strong desire to be more fearless, or have a greater purpose in your life. You can replace the week's subject you are skipping with a subject of your choice. A third way would be to choose the subjects you are most drawn to and work on them a week at a time. Either way, this book is for you, to change, to grow, to form new habits that will lead you to a happier, more joyful, more purposeful, and satisfying life.

Eight Empowering Steps to Change

❶ **Willingness.** First we look at the "Time for" subject for this week and ask ourselves if this is what I would like to concentrate on this week, or would I prefer to find another one that is more appropriate for what I am going through? Once we have made a decision and see the value in making a change, we still might not be ready to actually *make* the change. If we don't yet have the willingness but can see the value of making this change, we can ask for help, which leads us to pray.

❷ **We can pray for the willingness to make this change to whatever we believe is a power greater than ourselves.** Once we feel we have the willingness, we can move on.

❸ **We need an intention.** An intention is very powerful. It is the energy that takes us to our next step. Once we feel this intention, we can move on.

❹ **We make our commitment.** Our intention comes from our head. Our commitment comes from our heart. We feel this deeply. We want to change.

❺ **We can affirm our commitment.** We can create an affirmation such as: "It feels so good to know that God is giving me all that I need to be a forgiving person." Or, "I am becoming a fearless person today." Write your affirmation ten times a day for twenty-one days. You can see more about affirmations in my book, *Change Almost Anything in 21 Days*. Our affirmation leads to . . .

❻ **An action step.** The energy of our affirmation pushes us to an action step. For example, let's say our intention is to be fearless. We have become willing, and if we are not yet willing, we might pray for the willingness. Once we have willingness, we create an intention, which leads to our commitment, which leads to our affirmation, which leads us to an action. Our action step might be connecting to our breath until we feel peaceful. It might be repeating our affirmation until we are able to let go of our fear. Our action step might be to pray to have our fear removed. Whatever action step we take leads us to . . .

❼ **Practice.** The more we practice our action step, the more it becomes natural for us. It's like learning how to ride a bike. At first we might be wobbly and even fall a few times but the more we practice the easier it becomes. Soon we just hop on and pedal! Practice leads to . . .

❽ **Results.** We feel great! We have changed. No longer does our negative habit hold us back. We are free to be happy and full of joy.

Time for Beginning

There is excitement in new beginnings. We think every-thing will be different . . . fast! We have hope. We are inspired. What we often fail to understand or accept is that change usually takes time. It happens one step at a time. You might remember the old expression, "Inch by inch, it's a cinch. Yard by yard, it's hard." It's true!

How often have you tried something, found it difficult or that the change didn't happen as quickly as you thought it would and you just gave up? Please don't let this happen! That is why this book is based on practice . . . one week or longer at a time. *Time for Me* is designed for you to go at your own pace.

So let's make this first week one for getting ready for change. It will help you develop patience. It will help you get to know yourself better. It will help you be happier and more peaceful.

I congratulate you on your willingness!

This Week's Practice

I suggest you get a notebook and keep it exclusively for this entire year and this special life-changing project. You can use it to take notes, to journal, to save quotations or anything else you want to remember.

During this week be thoughtful of the changes you would like to make.

Make a list of these changes. Also make a list of the things you like and don't like about yourself. Add to these lists as you discover more things about yourself throughout the upcoming weeks.

There are two very important rules I hope you keep in mind as you go about your weeks:

1. Please accept everything you discover, and . . .

2. Do not judge anything.

If you notice yourself judging yourself, others or situations, and you probably will, practice letting go of all judgments. Begin to accept what is. Accept what you see about yourself, others, and your situations. Be sure not to judge even if and when you find yourself judging! In other words, don't judge your judging! This is a good rule to practice this week, this year and for the rest of your life. And finally, lighten up! Allow this practice to fill you with joy.

It feels so good to be taking time for me,
to learn about me, to discover and let go of where
I am stuck, and to move in a spiritual direction
of joy, peace, and purpose.

time for a bubble bath!

Time for Me

> "Time is a holy gift. Love yourself enough
> to give yourself more of it."
>
> —*Janet Conner*

Some of us, especially women, have been brought up to think that it is selfish to do things for ourselves. We have been taught we must think of others first. If we are married with children we must always put the kids and our spouse first. If we are in a relationship we put our partners before ourselves. If we ever do take time for ourselves we feel guilty.

13

And yet, how can we be complete if we don't take time for ourselves? How can we rest and renew and re-energize? How can we enjoy some of the things that are best done alone? How can we pray and meditate? How can we connect with God? How can we look deeply, get to know our true selves? Over the years I have had people tell me they didn't have time to meditate. The kids were too small. They had to let the dog out or the dog would bother them. They had company. They were needed!

"Put your oxygen mask on before you help someone else," the flight attendant announces before the plane takes off.

But even more important, it is perfectly okay to do something fun just for you. It's okay to take time to be alone, to take an hour or even a day or more here or there to fill your own needs, to go on a weekend retreat, to find joy in solitude.

This Week's Practice

Take some time this week to pause and consider this simple truth: taking care of yourself isn't "selfish." What will you lose if you and your needs are always put last?

Take some time this week to make a list of things that make you happy, things that you enjoy doing just for you. Then make sure you do at least one thing on that list each day, whether it's a bubble bath, reading a book, taking a walk, or sitting by the water. As the Nike slogan says, "Just do it!" Notice how you feel. If it is difficult to get away, can you perhaps ask someone to watch the kids for a short period of time? Is it hard to tell your partner you are taking time for you? Do you feel as if you have to ask for permission to do this?

Simply be aware of how you feel, without any judgment. If you feel guilty, do it anyway! This is a practice that is important to make a part of your life every week!

Take time each week to do the practice pages in this book. You'll find joy, peace, and purpose in your life!

I deserve to take time for me.
Or,
I have all the time I need today to take time for me.

Select one of these and write it ten times a day for twenty-one days. Feel it as you are writing it. Let these words fill you with power.

Time for Meditation

"Meditation is not a way of making
your mind quiet. It is a way of entering
into the quiet that is already there—buried
under the 50,000 thoughts the average
person thinks every day."

—*Deepak Chopra*

Meditation is a good way to begin our first weeks. Meditation teaches us how to live in the present moment, how to bring peace into our lives; it eases tension and stress, and helps us to get to know ourselves better. Many people think meditation connects us spiritually with what we believe in, whether it be the God of our understanding, universal energy, Allah, the Buddha within, or any power greater than ourselves. Peace Pilgrim wrote, "We spend a great deal of time telling God what we think should be done, and not enough time waiting in the stillness for God to tell us what to do." Even if you are an atheist or an agnostic, meditation can connect you with your inner spirit, your true self.

Meditation is a wonderful way to see how our minds work and how our minds are constantly busy with thoughts. We learn to notice our thoughts, and discover which thoughts create our suffering. We learn how to let go of our thoughts and thus begin to let go of our unhappiness and suffering.

There are hundreds of ways to meditate. For our practice this year I suggest you practice *mindfulness meditation*. Believe me, it's simple and you can't do it wrong! There are two parts to mindfulness and they are equally important.

The first is a daily sitting practice. Here is a very short and simple lesson in mindfulness, a way in which we can bring peace to ourselves in any moment. I suggest practicing meditation for a minimum of twenty minutes each day, preferably in the morning. It will change your life. If this feels like too much, begin with ten minutes and extend it as soon as you can to fifteen minutes, and then twenty. You can sit longer when you feel ready.

Find a comfortable place, either in a chair, or on a cushion, a meditation bench, or, as I practice it, sitting up in bed with three pillows behind me. Simply bring your awareness to the present moment.

I learned this practice more than thirty-six years ago. Larry Rosenberg, my teacher at that time, suggested that I sit for twenty minutes—whether I wanted to or not. I found the teachings so profound and life-changing that I chose to follow his advice and, as of this writing, I have not missed a day since then. I know myself well enough to know that if I miss one day, I will miss two and then three, and I might have a hard time getting back to it.

By practicing this twenty minutes in the morning, every day, you will learn how powerful your breath is. You will become more and more aware that you can turn to your breath at any time during the day to bring peace to your life.

People meditate for a variety of reasons. Many meditate to connect with the God of their understanding. Many combine meditation with prayer. People meditate to relieve stress, lower blood pressure, and to become more peaceful.

The Buddha was asked, "What have you gained from meditation?" He replied, "Nothing. However, let me tell you what I have lost: anger, anxiety, depression, insecurity, fear of old age and death."

We quiet our minds by learning to concentrate on our breathing in and out from our nose, or our chest rising and falling, or our stomach filling and emptying, or all three. We can concentrate on counting our in breath and out breath. We can concentrate on a word such as *peace,* or a phrase such as, "Breathing in, I know I am breathing in. Breathing out, I know I am breathing out." We are developing our capacity to concentrate.

Once we have learned to quiet our mind, it is good to set an *intention*. There is a Zen teaching that says, "The most important thing is remembering the most important thing."

My favorite definition of mindfulness, or *insight medita-tion* as it is also called, is from a brochure from the Insight Meditation Society in Barre, Massachusetts.

"Insight meditation is a simple and direct practice—the moment to moment investigation of the mind-body process through calm and focused awareness. Learning to experience from a place of stillness enables one to relate to life with less fear and less clinging. Seeing life as a constantly changing process, one begins to accept pleasure and pain, fear and joy, and all aspects of life with increasing equanimity and balance. As insight deepens, wisdom and compassion arise. Insight meditation is a way of seeing clearly the totality of one's being and experience. Growth in clarity brings about penetrating insight into the nature of who we are and increased peace in our daily lives."

The key word to my understanding of meditation here is awareness. Awareness is consciousness, insight, knowledge, and wakefulness. Its purpose is to be fully awake and aware in each moment, to discover the essence of who we are, to get in touch with all the blocks that keep us from touching our inner spirit and listening to the guidance of our soul.

"Four decades of brain research has proven that the brain is transformed by meditation, and now, newer evidence suggests that genetic output also improves with meditation. That is, the right genes get switched on and the wrong ones switched off," wrote Deepak Chopra, MD and Rudolph E. Tanzi, PhD in their book, *Super Brain*.

Some more benefits of meditations are:

- Slows the aging process
- Can improve memory and health
- Calms the nervous system
- Improves blood circulation
- Improves immune system
- Reduces insomnia and leads to better sleep
- Reduces anxiety and depression
- Increases concentration
- Supports addiction recovery
- Helps to keep memory sharp

- Lowers blood pressure
- Leads to fewer operations and fewer visits to the hospital
- Relieves worry

Buddhist nun, teacher, and author Pema Chödrön writes: "Everything in our lives can help us to wake up or to fall asleep, and basically it's up to us to let it wake us up."

This Week's Practice

Psychologist and Buddhist meditation proponent Tara Brach makes this suggestion to begin a meditation practice. "It is helpful to recall at the start of each sitting what matters to you, what draws you to meditate. Take a few moments to connect in a sincere way with your heart's aspiration. You might sense this as a prayer that in some way dedicates your practice to your own spiritual freedom, and that of all beings." This helps to develop the next step, that of insight. This is why it is often called insight meditation. Once we have quieted our minds, we can look deeply.

Sit comfortably, with your back as straight as possible. Let your entire body relax. Close your eyes very gently. If you wish, make an intention for this sitting such as intending to deepen your spirituality, or to bring more peace into your life and the lives of others. Bring your full awareness to your breath as you breathe in and out through your nose. You can say to yourself, *I am breathing in. I am breathing out. In. Out. Or, I am breathing in peace. I am breathing out tension. Peace. Tension.*

Simply notice whatever takes you away from your breathing: a thought, sound, itch, daydream, and acknowledge it by naming it. Then, very gently and without judgment, go back to your breathing.

The reason meditating first thing in the morning is recommended is that it makes you more aware for the rest of the day. If we meditate at noon our awareness will begin at noon. If we meditate after dinner, we'll only have a few hours of awareness. By meditating in the morning, you can carry this peace with you for the rest of the day.

It is said that twenty minutes of meditation is equivalent to two hours of sleep. So no matter what you have going on in the morning, you will not be tired if you get up twenty minutes earlier. I promise you, this is true!

There are hundreds, maybe even thousands of books on meditation and mindfulness. I've just given you a few suggestions; you can read more about it. I found getting a teacher and a group to sit with was very important for my understanding and growth. For many years after my first few classes I learned more by reading a variety of books. Eventually, I found a teacher and a group to sit with. After trying many kinds of meditation, I now follow the teaching Buddhist teacher and author Thich Nhat Hanh. My teache is Fred Eppsteiner. The group I sit with is called a *sangha*, simply a community of people who meditate together and support each other. My understanding of meditation grew much more quickly with a teacher and a group. You can also listen to CDs, go online and Google meditation, and learn so much more.

It feels so good to be a
daily meditator.

Time for Mindfulness

"Mindfulness is the aware,
balanced acceptance of the present experience.
It isn't more complicated than that.
It is opening to or receiving the present moment,
pleasant or unpleasant, just as it is, without
either clinging to it or rejecting it."

—*Sylvia Boorstein*

I am using the words meditation and mindfulness almost interchangeably as to me they are very much the same. Meditation teacher Richard Brady wrote, "I see meditation as an act that one does with intention, mindfulness as a way one encounters the present moment. In meditation one hopes to be mindful and may be for some of the time."

We practiced training our mind to return to where we want it to be. Last week we began practicing the first part of meditation, sitting. This is often called "training our monkey mind," because monkeys jump from branch to branch to branch, doing whatever they want to do. Until we train our mind to come back to where we want it to be, our mind does the same as the monkeys, jumping all over the place from past to present to future and back again, filled with our judgments, memories, and perceptions, real or imagined.

We became aware of how sometimes we are caught up in the same story we have told ourselves over and over again. This is the beginning of self-awareness. This is the beginning of how we can change our lives to create a happier, more joyful life. Meditation teacher and author Sharon Salzberg writes, "As your mind grows quieter and more spacious, you can begin to see self-defeating thought patterns for what they are, and open up to other, more positive options."

To me, the second part is mindfulness, becoming aware of our mind in the present moment—"off the cushion" as they say—in addition to our morning twenty minutes, during the rest of your day. It's a practice and will take time to become a habit. We practice noticing whether we are thinking about the past, the future or what we are experiencing now, this moment.

It's about noticing what we are feeling in each moment. It's discovering that what we think is what we feel. It's noticing whether we are judging, angry, fearful, calm, peaceful, whatever. Mindfulness is much more than self-examination. It is about being with whatever is in the moment and not running away from it, whether smelling a rose, listening deeply to a friend, watching a sunset, experiencing the pain of a break up or other bad news, or brushing our teeth. Meditation teacher Fred Eppsteiner tells us, "Mindfulness practice is a celebration of life in the present moment. It is not hard work!" And we can't do this wrong, either!

Practice being mindful this week. If this is new to you, don't be concerned if you are not mindful often. This takes time.

"Mindfulness is the miracle by which we can master and restore ourselves," author and teacher Thich Nhat Hanh suggests. "Whenever your mind becomes scattered, use your breath as the means to take hold of your mind again."

This Week's Practice

This week we are training ourselves to bring our awareness to the present moment. It is a practice that will grow until, eventually, it will be a natural part of our lives. Ironically, we usually begin by noticing we are not in the present moment!

We might become aware that while someone is talking to us we are not listening but instead thinking of what we are going to say next. We might be looking at a sunset and suddenly realize we aren't there at all but are thinking about our to-do list.

As soon as we notice our minds are somewhere else, wonderful! We are aware! We have begun! Now we simply bring our awareness to our breath. This keeps us in the present moment. Doing this as often as possible is our practice.

In a recent conference call, one of my teachers, Fred Eppsteiner, talked about how to live as an awakened mind in everyday life. He said that mindfulness is the capacity to be present to whatever happens right now. He suggested we do the following each day:

Set an intention to be mindful throughout the day.

See yourself doing this . . . visualize it.

Pause throughout the day.

Say, "I'm here to do this one thing. I'm here to be present to (drink tea, wash dishes, see a friend, or whatever you are doing)."

Use sticky notes, reminders, or *bells of mindfulness* on the Internet (Bells of mindfulness are tones rung at intervals throughout the day at meditation centers and at retreats, to remind us to stop, take three breaths, and re-center ourselves in the present. These are available as downloadable apps online and as online audio calendar reminders.)

I am finding peace by being in the moment,
and it feels so good.

prayer

Time for Prayer

"Prayer is sitting in the silence until it silences us,
choosing gratitude until we are grateful,
praising God until we ourselves are
a constant act of praise."

—*Fr. Richard Rohr, OFM*

Morning prayer and meditation is, to me, a similar connection with my higher self, my inner spirit, my Higher Power, God. I become willing to open myself up to the deepest place within me and connect with all the energies of the universe, whatever they might be. I truly have no idea who or what God is, or to what I am praying. But I do know that there is power and energy in the universe greater than myself and, when I pray, I make a connection to the power and energy.

I take the time to pray, even if I don't know to whom or what I am praying. I connect in the morning by asking, and again in the evening by being grateful.

I know that the power I had during the day did not come solely from myself. But prayers do not always give us the answers we seek. Nelia Gardner White advises us, "Some people just don't seem to realize when they're moaning about not getting prayers answered that 'no' is the answer." Another saying suggests that God answers "yes, no, or I have another answer for you." When we seek the knowledge of God's will for us and the power to carry it out, we get the courage and strength we need to get through whatever happens in our lives.

It is said that in prayer we talk to God and in meditation we listen. When I first tried to get sober, people strongly suggested I pray to God for help. I was an agnostic at the time. I thought, *Maybe there is, maybe there isn't a God. We'll never know.* So I asked, "God, if you're not there it doesn't matter and if you are, you'll understand, but please keep me away from a drink and a pill and a desire for a drink and a pill today." And later, "Please take away my desire to drink." And the miracle happened! That was forty-two years ago and

I have not had a drink since. I came to believe in a power greater than myself and now I pray every day. It worked! The miracle happened. I became a deeply grateful believer. I personally pray after I meditate, as that is when I feel more spiritually connected. See what works best for you. An Eric S. Fromme quote helped me: "Man is finite and God is infinite and therefore man will never know God."

God is still a mystery to me but my relationship with God has grown. I came to see God as a power for good and love. For me, God is energy, a force, a power for good and love to turn to in times of trouble, and to thank often during the day. Keeping it very simple, I merely need to know there is a power greater than myself and that I am not in charge of the universe.

I agree with author, psychotherapist, and retreat leader Sylvia Boorstein who says that she "likes" prayers. She doesn't know what she's praying to or if she's praying to anything. She just likes praying. "I know I can connect with this power greater than myself at any time, and that gives me great comfort."

So whatever you believe God is or isn't, just knowing that there is a power greater than you, and you are not God, is enough.

Scientific studies have proven that prayers aid healing. One recent study followed a group of cancer patients who were divided into three groups, one on medication, one on placebos, and one where individuals were prayed for regularly by family or friends or a church group. The group that people prayed for had a higher recovery rate than the other two groups.

My friend and co-retreat leader Joann Malone wrote, "Now, time for prayer is anytime, all day, that I lift my mind and heart to the Ultimate, that I realize my connection to every other human being, to all of life. Prayer is no longer merely asking for something I need but a powerful energy that transforms me."

This Week's Practice

I have collected many prayers over the years. They set a beautiful tone for me. Here are four others I particularly like:

"I dedicate all my actions of this day to the benefit of all living beings." The Dalai Lama says this every morning.

A Day's Plan: please direct my thinking. From the *Big Book of Alcoholics Anonymous*, on page 86: "On awakening let us think about the twenty-four hours ahead. We consider our plans for the day. Before we begin, we ask God to direct our thinking, especially asking that it be divorced from self-pity, dishonest or self-seeking motives."

Thich Nhat Hanh prays, "Waking up in the morning I smile, twenty-four brand-new hours are before me. I vow to live fully in each moment and to look at all beings with eyes of compassion."

And finally, from Shantideva, "I have attained this extraordinary and precious human birth. This human birth I will use wisely for my own awakening and for the greatest benefit of all living beings."

Martin Luther suggests on a busy day we affirm, "I have so much to do today that I shall spend the first three hours in prayer."

You can begin by saying any prayer you are comfortable with. Collect your own.

I am connecting with my Higher Power
every morning during meditation and prayer;
this fills my heart with a lightness and joy
I carry with me throughout the day. It feels so good
to know that if I lose this connection I can
rekindle it anytime with a new prayer.

Time for Intention

> "Intentions set into process every
> aspect of your life."
>
> —*Gary Zukav*

Change begins with willingness. It's obvious that we won't make conscious changes in our lives unless we are willing to make them. Of course there will always be changes that happen in our lives in the process of life itself. Change is constant. We are talking here about the changes *we want to make* to have more joy and less suffering in our lives.

Making an intention gives energy to our willingness. It is an action step, as in, "I intend." Joseph Goldstein writes,

"Volition is the mental urge or signal which precedes an action."

In *The Seat of the Soul*, Gary Zukav gives us the following example of intending to change your job. "As the intention to leave your present job emerges into your consciousness, you begin to open yourself up to the possibility of working somewhere else or doing something else. You begin to feel less and less at home with what you are doing. Your higher self has begun the search for your next job."

This Week's Practice

A Course in Miracles tells us our good intentions are not enough. Our willingness is everything. Therefore, let's take an action step this week to combine our intentions with our willingness.

We begin with something we want to add, reduce, change, or let go of in our life. We intend to make it happen. And, with the following steps, we learn we can make the change.

Studies have shown that the simple act of taking the time to write out your goals will dramatically increase the likelihood of achieving those goals!

1. First, create an intention. It can be to be a daily meditator, to find a new job, to be a better partner—anything

that is on the top of your mind for you right now. You can have more than one intention, but I would suggest not too many. Make an intention to meditate at least once each morning and to be as mindful as you can throughout the day. To help you develop the practice of meditation I would suggest you have this on the top of your list until it becomes a regular habit.

2. Once you have decided on your intention, write it down.
3. Visualize your intention coming true. How would you look? How would you feel?
4. Sit quietly in meditation. Ask yourself, what are the action steps I need to take to succeed in this intention?

Write down these four steps for each intention.

The following week on affirmations will help your intentions come into fruition.

I feel inspiration, power,
and strength pouring through me as
I write my intention today.

Time for Morning

"Each morning we are born again.
What we do with today is what matters most."

—*The Buddha*

The morning is a great time to set the tone for the upcoming day, and yet many of us wake up with a to-do list in our head, our minds immediately rushing to figure out how to accomplish it all. Others feel an immediate fear or dread of getting through the day, or of a particular fearful event or circumstance they are facing that day. I used to have a bit of both, sometimes more, sometimes less, but some dread or feeling of discomfort was always there. Before knowing anything about meditation, and while we were beginning a halfway house for recovering alcoholic women, I would wake up around 5 AM and my mind would go over and over the budget, trying to figure out how to have enough money for food and rent. My busy mind wouldn't let me fall back asleep. Once I learned about meditation and mindfulness, I began breathing in peace and breathing out tension, and was able to fall back to sleep for a few hours. What a difference having this sleep made in my day!

Meditation has been a part of my morning ritual for more than thirty-six years. It is a spiritual practice that brings me closer to the God of my understanding, helps me to live more in the now, and helps me to be aware of my thoughts that create my suffering. To see more about meditation, look at the week for Time for Meditation.

This Week's Practice

On the light side (if you will excuse the pun), think of this quote by Robert Brault if you want to smile when you wake up: "There would be a lot more optimists if it weren't for the rise-and-shine requirement."

When you do wake up feeling overwhelmed, with a long to-do list facing you, here are a few ways to come to a place of peace. You can say: "God gives me all the time and energy I need to do God's work."

Author Shakti Gawain suggests saying, "Everything is flowing easily and effortlessly." I've used this for years and it works beautifully!

My friend and author Nicki Burton suggests we go on a "yes" fast. We stop saying "yes" when we feel overwhelmed by our to-do list. She tells herself to say "no" to the next six things that come up for her, and she keeps a list. It gives her immediate stress relief knowing that she's taking a positive action going forward to help herself, and saying no is a good practice. It means she's saying yes to the things that are more important.

Once you have cleared your mind from your overwhelming to-do list, I suggest reading something inspirational. This sets your thinking on a spiritual path. Since it is said that prayer is asking and meditation is listening, logically, you might want to pray before or after you meditate. Try both ways and see what way works best for you.

A wonderful morning practice is creating the habit of smiling upon awakening.

It immediately prevents tension and worry from creeping in. Then expect something good to happen to you today.

Another is adding gratitude to your morning routine. Even before opening your eyes, get into the habit of smiling and thinking of a few things or people for whom you are grateful.

Set an intention. How do you intend to spend your day? To be helpful, happy, grateful? See the pages for Time for Intention for more ideas.

By practicing these simple suggestions, you'll be amazed at the results in a short time. Let the following poem be an inspiration for you:

Thousands of Reasons

by Doe Zantamata

If every morning,
You can find a reason to say,
"Yes, it's going to be a beautiful day."
And every night, you find a reason to say,
"Yes, it was a beautiful day."
Then one day,
You'll look back and easily say,
"Yes . . . it was a beautiful life."

*I begin my day with quiet time, finding peace
and serenity in my meditation. I carry those feelings
with me wherever I am. If I get stressed or fearful,
I can stop and spend a few minutes with my
breath and regain my serenity.*

*It is such a joy to know that I can make any day
happy by my attitude in the morning.*

Time for Night

"Another day's over. And the earth
unconditionally holds us on her heart,
rocking us gently to sleep."

—*Unknown Sage*

How often we are kept awake at night with the thoughts and stories going round and round in our heads. She did this. He did that. I didn't do this. I did that. Why did this happen? What if this happens? And on and on. We might go over our to-do list and think of all the things we haven't done on it. Or think of conversations we had with people and wonder why we said this and not that.

Rick Hanson, PhD, a neuropsychologist and author, writes that, for our survival, our brain was wired in such a way when it evolved to learn quickly from bad experiences. That's why it is easier for us to ruminate over hurt feelings rather than bask in the warmth of feeling loved.

This Week's Practice

Just as you read in the pages for morning, when your head is on the pillow each night, smile and expect something good to happen to you tomorrow. If you should wake up during the night, smile. Expect something good to happen to you the next day. When you wake up in the morning, smile. Expect something good to happen to you today. It is also suggested to begin breathing in peace and breathing out tension. Usually this will help you fall asleep.

There are many other good suggestions in the morning practice. Ending the day as we began it, with gratitude for people and things in our lives, can bring us a wonderful sense of peace and leave a smile on our face. Recovery programs suggest before we go to bed, we examine our entire day, seeing if perhaps we need to make amends for any harm we have done.

Author Neale Donald Walsch has a suggestion about receiving an answer to something you have been waiting for.

He writes that what we want to know is already inside of us. He suggests we simply write our question, condition, or problem down on a piece of paper before we go to sleep, then pick up the paper in the morning and compose a calm, wisdom-filled response. Don't be surprised if you surprise yourself with the answer you receive.

Changing a thought that is negative or self-critical can be very helpful. In his book *Hardwiring Happiness*, Dr. Rick Hanson has a wonderful suggestion on how to build new neural structures in our brain that attract happiness, love, confidence, and peace. When we stay with a positive experience a few extra seconds we form a lasting neural structure. He calls this "taking in the good."

"As your positive mental states become positive neural traits, you'll gradually rest in a happiness that emerges naturally inside of you," Hanson says. When you do this during the day, you can recall these moments at night, breathe in the good feelings, smile, and fall asleep. You'll find more helpful suggestions when you come to the week on neuroplasticity.

I smile as I turn over all my critical,
negative, judgmental thoughts, and let myself
rest in the peace of positive,
happy memories.

Time for Breathing

"Breath is the bridge which connects
life to consciousness, which unites your body to
your thoughts. Whenever your mind becomes
scattered, use your breath as the means to
take hold of your mind again."

—*Thich Nhat Hanh*

Being aware of your breath can be the simplest, easiest way
to slow down, reduce stress, connect spiritually, avoid
arguments, eliminate fear, connect with another person, and
feel peaceful. Taking three breaths stops any negative emotion and brings you into this moment . . . right now. Anger

leaves before you have time to say anything you will regret later. Your mind becomes clear. It's a wonderful feeling!

The more you practice your sitting meditation in the morning, the quicker you will be aware during the rest of your day and will remember to come back to the moment by being with your breath. You can also become aware of the stories you tell yourself that create your suffering.

Meditation teacher and friend Bill Menza wrote, "To train and tame the mind to have pure awareness we can begin with being fully aware of your breathing in and out. This is where most beginning meditators start. You might even use a mantra (a small focused poem) to help you to have 100 percent concentration on your breathing. For example, as you breathe in you say to yourself: 'I know I am breathing in.' And when you breathe out you say: 'I know I am breathing out.'"

One mind-training teacher said that, "Doing this as much as you can for a year will bring you more calmness and peace than all the courses and studying you might do for the same period. And it's free!"

One day I was driving to a meeting. The road I took that morning was filled with cars going in and out of the lanes, fast and slow. I could feel myself getting more and more uptight. I was about to yell but I stopped. I breathed in and out three times. *Ahhh* . . . peace. I smiled. It works every time. Later in the day I took my dog out for a walk. My mind

began to rush over all the things I still had to do. I stopped.
I breathed in and out three times. My thoughts stopped and
I was just with my dog, the flowers, the trees. No thoughts.
Nothing but this moment. Again . . . peace!

It amazes me every time! Peter Matthiessen writes, "In
this very breath that we now take lies the secret that all great
teachers try to tell us."

This Week's Practice

Joanne Friday, my first meditation teacher, once signed
her email: "With much love and the deep peace of three conscious breaths for you."

How very wonderful! I offer that to you this week. You
don't have to change your breathing by making it deeper or
slower, or do alternate nostril breathing as is suggested in
some yoga groups. Just be conscious of your breath as you
breathe in and out three times. You will be amazed at the
change it can make in your mood and emotions.

*My Higher Power is helping me to remember
to stop and breathe in and out three times whenever
I am stressed or fearful. It feels so good to bring my
awareness to my breath every time I want peace.*

Time for Observing

"Our brain takes its shape from what
the mind rests upon."

—*Rick Hanson, PhD*

As we become more and more mindful, we see we are really observing the present moment more often. We are noticing, watching, seeing what is here and what we are feeling right now. Author and neuroscientist Rick Hanson tells us how our experience matters. He explains that our experience of happiness, worry, love, and anxiety can make real changes in our neural networks. "If our thoughts are of self-criticism, worries, hurts, and stress, our brain will be shaped into greater reactivity. We will have a tendency toward anxiety and depression, and inclination toward anger, sadness, and guilt. On the other hand, if our thoughts are on good events and conditions, pleasant feelings, good intentions, etc., our brains are hardwired with strength, resilience, and happiness. We'll have a realistic outlook, a positive mood, and a sense of self-worth. We can deliberately prolong and even create the experiences that will reshape our brain for the better."

If we are looking at a flower there is nothing else but the flower in our mind. Pure mindfulness is not even having any thoughts about the flower. We stop thinking how pretty it might be or whether or not we like the color. We are simply one with the flower. We are observing our senses, noticing the aromas, the sounds, the sensations, the sights and tastes of the present moment.

This is true with feelings as well. If, when seeing the flower, a memory is triggered from a time when someone dear to us gave us a flower like this and we are flooded with love, we are aware of the feeling. Let's say, for example, we see the same make of car that once sideswiped us and we are filled with fear. We don't try to push away the fear but stay mindful of the feeling and let it pass. When we have strong feelings in us, we observe the strong feelings. How many times have we tried to run away from strong, painful, unpleasant feelings, only to have them creep up on us at a later time? By observing them, being with them, they fade and the feelings of the next moment arise.

So how do we handle the unpleasant ones? The ones that linger? Observing might not be enough. We have to accept them as well. And then change them. This changes our brain. This is when we find peace. Thich Nhat Hanh teaches us to use what are called *gathas*. The Plum Village Practice Center explains that gathas are short verses that help us practice mindfulness in our daily activities. For example, if we are angry, we don't try to push the feeling away or try to ignore it. We observe the anger and perhaps take a walk so as not to say anything we might regret. We can say to ourselves: *Breathing in I know the anger is in me. Breathing out I know this feeling is unpleasant.* This helps us accept the feeling. And then after a while we can say: *Breathing in I feel calm. Breathing out I am strong enough to take care of this anger.* Without going into our mind, our thoughts, or our stories about the feeling, we *experience* the feeling. We observe it. We let it pass.

Observing our thoughts can tell us a great deal about ourselves. Author Deepak Chopra, MD, was inspired in graduate school when he heard: "If you want to know what your thoughts were like in the past, look at your body today. If you want to know what your body will look like in the future, look at your thoughts today." A powerful lesson here!

For more difficult feelings that won't go away we might look more deeply into their source. But that practice is for next week.

This Week's Practice

The more we practice mindfulness, the easier observing our feelings will become. It helps to picture a stop sign. As feelings arise, just be with them. Don't use the multitude of ways to try to escape them. Eating a candy bar, for example, might be pleasant at first but the feelings are still there when the candy bar is gone.

Stopping, observing, feeling, and accepting are usually enough. Remember, this is a practice and takes time. You couldn't ride a bicycle the first time you got on it, could you? A seed recently planted takes care and time to grow.

It is so peaceful to let go of stories
and judgments and preconceived ideas,
and simply be in this moment.

Time for Neuroplasticity

"Neuroplasticity is our ability to change our mind, to change ourselves and to change our perception of the world around us . . . we have to change how the brain automatically and habitually works. The ability to make our brain forgo its habitual internal wiring and fire new patterns and combinations is how neuroplasticity allows us to change."

—*Joe Dispenza, DC*

It's exciting to know our brains are not hardwired, as has been thought until very recently. Scientists have now proven that we have the ability to rewire and create new neural circuits—at any age! Alex Lerner, MD, tells us, "the brain's neuro-function has both hardwiring and software. The brain is the hardwiring and the mind is the application of software. The mind can change or modify the hardwiring of old neural networks in order to create new neural networks or programs in the brain with our thoughts." It's exciting to know that our thoughts can rewire our brain.

As we have been practicing, mindfulness helps us to be aware of our thoughts. We are learning to distinguish them between healthy and unhealthy, joy-producing and stress-producing. The longer we practice mindfulness the more quickly we will be able to turn a negative thought into a positive one. The more we do this, we lessen our automatic reactions that produce stress and suffering, and increase reactions that produce joy, compassion, love, and equanimity.

Imagine that you have been driving through mud over and over again. Each time you drive over the same place, the ruts in the mud get deeper and deeper. Now imagine that you take a different road. The new drive begins to create deeper and deeper ruts in the road while the old ruts begin to disappear because of lack of use.

This is exactly what happens with our thoughts. Before knowing any better, our thoughts were triggered automatically. For example, let's imagine you smell chicken soup. If your mother had left a potholder on the stove that caught fire while she was heating your chicken soup, fear would automatically come up. If she lovingly cooked chicken soup for you while you were sick, feelings of love would come up for you. By being mindful of your thoughts you can see that your reaction to the smell is triggered from the past. You can bring your awareness to this moment, now, and smell the chicken soup. Your mind will react to what you are feeling in the present moment. You will either like the soup or not, depending on the current experience.

Let's say a driver cuts you off. Anger immediately comes up for you. "How dare he!" Breathe. Say *shhhh* to yourself. This gives you space away from the anger. Breathe in deeply and send the driver thoughts of peace or loving-kindness. Your immediate reaction is instantly replaced by peace—just because you have changed your thought. And if you do this a number of times, the anger reaction will recede and come up for you less and less often!

New thoughts make new chemicals. When we change our mind it alters the chemical messages to our body. Feel-good chemicals are stimulated and flow through our body. When we learn something new or react in a new way, the brain makes new synaptic connections to form new neural patterns or networks. We're actually rewiring our brain. It's really this easy!

Scientists have also found that the simple step of giving an older person a pet to take care of instills more willingness to live. What really invigorates an older person is having a new purpose and something new to love. These both stimulate new neurons in the brain and new feel-good chemicals in our body.

This Week's Practice

There is a saying that where attention goes, energy flows. This week let's practice putting our attention toward things that make us feel good such as love and joy and compassion.

There's also a saying that is very important: "It's the second thought that counts." This means that the first thought will still come up, the one that is wired in our brain from our reactions. We can stay with it or change it; our choice. So be aware of all your reactions this week. Notice them as if you were detached from them, as if you were the observer or the witness of your thoughts and reactions. And if the reactions are negative, create a new thought right away.

You can ask yourself: *does this thought make me happy?* And if the answer is no, create a new one. Practice this over and over again until it becomes a lifetime habit. Alex Lerner reminds us of the "old" adage in twenty-first century neuroscience: "neurons that fire together, wire together."

Here's a good practice for changing your brain, (originally published in my book *Wrinkles Don't Hurt: The Joy of Aging Mindfully*, the entry for March 24):

Imagine new neural pathways forming in your brain as you think positive thoughts.

Imagine new neural pathways forming in your brain as you try something new.

Imagine the happiness part of your brain getting larger as you practice mindfulness.

Imagine your heart opening as your willingness to forgive someone expands. And feel the joy as your capacity for generosity grows in you . . . one day at a time.

It's a joy to know that I can change
my thoughts and change my brain at
any age and become a happier,
healthier person.

Time for Peace

Greater in combat than the person who
conquers a thousand times a thousand people
is the person who conquers himself.

—*The Buddha*

As we have been learning, our thoughts create our feelings. When we truly understand the implications of this, we can experience a tremendous freedom. No longer do we need to be victims of either other people or of our past. We see that we can be responsible for our lives! We can choose to think thoughts that create peace, happiness, love, and compassion rather than anger, fear, or bitterness.

As we grow in our ability to be mindful of how we speak to ourselves, we discover whether we are being a judge, critic, friend, or cheerleader. This takes practice, and it's important to remember we are moving toward progress, not perfection. At first, the voice of our inner judge or critic might be the loudest we hear because they have been in charge for so many years. Once we get in touch with this tendency, we can choose to allow that voice to evaporate, replacing it with more loving and compassionate self-talk.

Pema Chödrön tells us that, "The peace that we're looking for is not peace that crumbles as soon as there is difficulty or chaos. The way to experience it is to build on the foundation of unconditional openness to all that arises. Peace isn't an experience free of challenges, free of rough and smooth; it's an experience that's expansive enough to include all that arises without feeling threatened."

Are we at war with our weight, food, drugs, or alcohol? Do we spend more than we can afford? Are we going back and forth between should I or shouldn't I? Do we struggle with fear versus faith, selfishness versus generosity and so forth? It is helpful to observe whatever it is with which we struggle. As we become willing to resolve our own inner struggles, outside issues often resolve themselves. Each time we are willing to look at our own issues, we come to a greater understanding of the conflicts others have.

If we can't stop the battles in our minds, how can we expect to stop the battles in the world? We need to begin with ourselves and first understand our own personal conflicts.

We can't always be peaceful and loving even when we have the best intentions. Unexpected events can stimulate fear. Old buttons can be pushed. A burst of anger can lead to words we later regret. No emotion is right or wrong; all emotions are natural.

It is so important that we are gentle with ourselves and accept our emotions without judgment, no matter what is going on. Acceptance releases negative energy.

Just knowing that there are times that we are powerless over our feelings can be the beginning of peace. Turning over our emotions to a power greater than ourselves and trusting that God can and will do for us what we cannot do for ourselves, can bring us peace.

"When you find peace within yourself, you become the kind of person who can live at peace with others," wrote Peace Pilgrim.

This Week's Practice

It's good to take time each day to get away from the turmoil of our daily routines and rest in solitude. Even five minutes alone can help us to reach a place deep inside ourselves, where we can find peace.

Mindfulness can bring peace to us in any moment. Your morning practice can start your day peacefully. Meditating a few minutes any other time during the day can reinforce peace.

Know that whatever is going on in your life, you can feel peaceful. This gift awaits you in each moment. The more you practice it, the more you will remember to use it in times of stress and anxiety.

During your morning meditation or any time during the day when you feel stressed or negative or fearful, say to yourself: *Breathing in peace, breathing out tension.* Try it now. It feels good.

What else can you do to have more peace in your heart?

Is there someone you need to forgive?

Is your to-do list too long?

Do you feel stuck without a purpose?

Is there something you have been putting off?

Are you meditating every day?

Are you praying every day?

Are you learning something new to improve your memory?

Are you exercising?

Is there something else you can do?

Mel Weldon wrote, "My mind is a garden. My thoughts are the seeds. My harvest will be either flower or weeds." It's up to us! Remember, we can create our own peace and happiness. We don't need to wait to have someone else do it for us! Choose to harvest flowers.

> *Today I am taking time alone to find*
> *inner peace, to get to know myself better and*
> *to see that I am becoming the beautiful*
> *person God intended me to be.*

> *Today I am taking time to*
> *bring my awareness to my breath,*
> *choosing to find peace in*
> *each moment.*

Time for Journaling

"Find your own quiet center of life, and
write from that to the world."

—*Sarah Orne Jewett*

Journaling is a very private and personal experience that will probably feel different from day to day, year to year. There are times when I can't wait to begin writing in my journal. Words bubble up inside of me, eager to pour out. As soon as my pen touches the paper it flows non-stop until whatever it was that had been going on deep within me has expressed itself completely. Other times, each word can be a struggle because I'm not quite sure what I am feeling and it takes a while to get started.

Journaling is a very special and intimate time we take for ourselves. I have frequently turned to my journal over the years as a vehicle to express what was going on in my life. Sometimes I've used it to record significant events, but most often I have journaled to help me through difficult times. My journal carries me from one place to another, moves me, helps me become unstuck. At various times it has served as a bridge, allowing me to leave my pain behind so that I could move on, and it has been a safe container for my feelings.

I reached for it in the days after my son died. Looking back later through my journal, I cannot believe the intensity of the pain I felt at that time of my life. I came to understand that I was writing words I was incapable of saying aloud. It served as a way to clear the massive, uninvited, intrusive, and heavy burden that stuck inside my gut and my chest and my throat. Putting words to the horror that I was feeling served to move around the energy of the pain so that it could be released and I could be free to go through the motions of doing whatever was required of me each day. Some days the words just poured out while other days I just stared at the paper without any words at all. On these days, I simply wrote a few words such as, "terrible day," or "Here I go again." I knew instinctively the natural inclination of my soul and followed it. My journal was a safe place to turn, a trusted friend. It gave me great comfort and was a wonderful release.

I was fortunate enough to know that whatever was going on inside me needed to be expressed or it would damage me mentally, physically, and spiritually. At another level, the writer part of me also knew that when I became ready to share it with others, it would help them, too.

To express how we feel helps us along the path of healing. Let the words and feelings come out without concern for grammar or form, or even if it doesn't make any sense. Let these pages serve as a safe container for your thoughts and feelings. You never have to share these words with anyone. It is up to you.

Elbert Hubbard writes, "The cure for grief is motion." Journaling can be just the motion we need to move us through any unresolved grief. Journaling helps us to maintain a perspective in our life in the midst of movement and change. We can look at where we are stuck and where we repeat patterns that get us in trouble.

There are other great values of journaling. It slows us down, for one thing. The act of picking up a pen or pencil, placing it on the page, and transferring the thoughts that are in our minds to that piece of paper places us directly in the present moment. We can feel the pen and the paper, hear their sounds, smell their uniqueness. Our minds are focused instead of racing off into other directions.

Yet journaling does not always have to be written by hand in a notebook. I have found that when I am short of time or filled with what feels like a million things to say, I turn on the computer where I can write faster and let it flow, whatever I'm feeling, whatever is coming up for me. It's a wonderful release and a way to get clarity in a time of confusion.

This Week's Practice

Find a place where you feel safe, a quiet space far enough away from everyone so that there are no interruptions. You might begin with a few minutes of meditation to find a quiet place within you. Invite your Higher Power, God, or spirit in and let yourself feel the safety and peace of this moment. Sit quietly for a few moments until you feel calm and relaxed.

We can do many things to create our own personal space. For example:

Light a candle or many candles

Play mood music

Have a favorite stuffed animal nearby

Have a pet with you for company

Burn incense

Ask the family or whoever you live with for privacy

Turn your phone off

Put a Do Not Disturb sign on the door

Use a book or notebook that feels good to you and keep it in a safe place.

Write a focusing statement such as:

I know my Higher Power is with me as I write.

Kathleen Adams, in her book *The Way of the Journal: A Journal Therapy Workbook for Healing,* suggests that we put on the front page of our journal:

STOP! THIS IS THE PERSONAL JOURNAL OF _____. DO NOT READ ANY FURTHER UNLESS YOU HAVE BEEN GIVEN PERMISSION.

She also suggests that we write the word *breathe* at the top of every page and stop writing when we feel overwhelmed.

Write something expressing yourself every morning, even if it is only a sentence or two, a thought or two. This will get you into the habit of making this a regular practice in your life.

I am willing to express all the feelings that have been holding me back from living the joyous and authentic life I was meant to live. I can search deep within me and write them down in my journal, knowing every step takes me to healing and freedom.

i am intelligent
i can, i can, i can
moving forward today

Time for Affirmations

"Thoughts of your mind have made you what
you are and thoughts of your mind will make you
what you become from this day forward."

—*Catherine Ponder*

I spent so many years, from childhood to my late thirties, stuck with tapes such as "I'm not good enough," "I'll never be accepted," and later, "Who would want to hear me speak? Others are so much better than me!" It was just who I was, or at least that's what I thought of me. And then I got into recovery and learned about meditation and mindfulness. I began to wake up to the voices in my head and learn they were not me but messages that came to me much earlier. Soon I learned about affirmations and how we can actually change the messages in our brain. And later I began learning about neuroplasticity, the fact that our brain was actually plastic and we could change our brain by changing our thoughts. This came from new research by scientists beginning in the mid 1970's. All this was life-changing for me and I became what felt like a new person.

As we learn to quiet our minds and listen to our self-talk, we become aware of the words we tell ourselves. We begin to see that these words have the power to make us feel good or bad, confident or fearful, positive or negative. It has been scientifically proven that the words we tell ourselves can even make us healthy or sick. Most of our illnesses come from stress which comes from perceiving what is happening in our life as negative or fearful.

Negative words block us from moving forward. Here are some examples:

When I say, "I can't," then I can't. I'll feel inadequate.

When I say, "I'll never be able to _____," then I never will be able to _____. I'll feel incapable.

When I say, "I haven't enough time," then I'm all about not having enough time. I'll feel rushed and full of anxiety.

On the positive side:

When I say, "I am terrific just the way I am!" I feel energized, enthused, upbeat.

When I say, "I am feeling peace in this very moment," I feel serene and peaceful.

When I say, "I have all the intelligence I need to pass this test," I feel confident and strong.

Once we realize that how we feel is a direct result of how we talk to ourselves, or a reaction to what people say to us then we have a new and powerful tool to change how we feel. We have a *choice*. Affirmations are powerful tools to help us break away from our past messages. By changing our thinking we can change our attitude, which helps us change our actions, so we can change our lives.

Affirmations are so simple that many people think they are too simple to work. I have used them and have taught them to thousands of people and the results have been amazing.

Shakti Gawain, author of *Creative Visualizations*, wrote that when completing an affirmation, know or say, "This or something better for all concerned is manifesting itself for me." It is not always true that we know what is best for ourselves, and if we learn to wait and listen, the right answer will be there.

I received a call from a young woman who had attended one of my workshops. She told the following story: she had been out of control with her spending and had been too afraid to tell anyone. Purchases were hidden under her bed, never looked at once they were home. Closets were full of new, unworn clothes. If she was depressed or upset, or felt anything she didn't want to feel, shopping gave her the adrenaline rush she needed, or thought she needed, to get through the rough time, to lift her mood. She was close to deep financial trouble and she was physically sick with worry and shame.

She never shared this obsession with anyone for fear they would try to stop her. After my workshop she took my suggestion and quietly began to write ten times each day: "I have everything I need today!"

A few days later some friends called and asked her if she wanted to go shopping. They went to the mall and looked at the new fall clothes. "Isn't that stunning!" said one of the friends. "Yes," she responded quietly, "but I have everything I need today." She couldn't believe those words came out of her mouth. She continued to write her affirmation until she had completed twenty-one days. In the end, she was able to talk about her shopping addiction with her husband and, in time, put her finances back in order.

Affirmations work. As I wrote in my book, *Change Almost Anything in 21 Days*, affirmations must consist of five parts. They must be:

1. Positive. Say "I am confident today," not, "I am no longer negative."
2. Said and felt with passion and power. "I am confident today!"

3. Kept in the present moment. Say, "I am confident today," not, "I will be confident."

4. Possible. I could not affirm that I am a famous singer as I am tone deaf; but I could affirm that I am a successful writer.

5. Personal. We cannot affirm for someone else, only ourselves.

Many years ago I read *Psycho-Cybernetics* by Maxwell Maltz. Dr. Maltz was a plastic surgeon who operated primarily on faces. He wrote that he noticed a sudden and dramatic change in personality in most cases when he operated on "a person who had a conspicuously ugly face, or some 'freakish' feature. Usually there was a rise in self-esteem and self-confidence in twenty-one days. Those who didn't change continued to feel just as if they still had an ugly face."

Dr. Maltz wrote that it usually requires twenty-one days to effect any perceptible change, and he suggests reserving all judgment for twenty-one days. Though no one knows exactly why this number holds such power over mind and body, Dr. Maltz and others have observed this phenomenon.

This is why I suggest you write your affirmation for twenty-one days and witness for yourself the miraculous changes that happen in your life. The twenty-one days must be consecutive. If you miss a day in the series, you must start over again for it to be effective.

One way to find the right affirmation for yourself is to think about something you would like to change in your life, something you might want to add or let go. Close your eyes and imagine this goal as if it is real. Imagine the change has already happened for you. How would you feel? Now think of all the reasons why this change cannot occur. For example, perhaps you would like to be a writer. You might tell yourself that you are stupid or can't spell.

Now write a positive affirmation, turning around the negative statement that blocks you from making this change in your life. Make sure it has the five ingredients from the section before this one, i.e., it must be positive, powerful, in the present moment, possible, and personal. Your affirmation can be, "I am writing a successful book today."

Perhaps you would like to spend more time in solitude but think you don't have enough time. Your affirmation can be, "I have all the time I need to take some time for me today," or, "God gives me all the time I need to take some time for me today." I often like including "God" or "all the energies of the universe" in my affirmations because that feels more powerful to me.

Affirmations help us to open up to positive energy and attract us to that which we would like to accomplish. They can be very powerfully combined with meditation. You can record your affirmations. Meditate for as long as you wish and when you feel quiet and peaceful, play them. Affirmations are very effective when we hear them in a deeper state of consciousness, as we are when we are meditating.

Shakti Gawain wrote, "What we create within is always mirrored outside of us. That is the law of the universe."

Remember, you can add, "God is helping me" at the beginning of the affirmation such as:

"God is helping me find the perfect job for me today."

You can also add,

"It feels so good to know that God is helping me find the perfect job for me today."

Here are some other examples of affirmations:

I am terrific just the way I am!

All the energies of the universe are guiding me to my next step.

I am eating healthy food to keep me at a healthy weight.

I am loving and lovable.

I have all the time I need to take time for me today.

Time for Expressing Yourself

"Every impulse we strangle
will only poison us."

—*Oscar Wilde*

One of the most important lessons you can learn this
year is not to hold in anything that is disturbing to
you. This only creates suffering. The more we hold back, the
more we block ourselves from really being alive, from living
in the moment, from being free and being happy. I learned
this many years ago. I made a pact with myself that I would

express, either to someone I trusted, or to paper, within twenty-four hours, anything that disturbed me. Doing this has changed my life. If I wasn't ready to talk about something bothering me I would journal about it. After writing about it, if it still bothered me, I would find someone I could trust and talk to that person.

Last week we practiced journaling. I hope you will make it a lifetime practice along with meditation, mindfulness, and expressing whatever is bothering you.

These early weeks are very important for you to form a solid base for your year and thus for your life.

This Week's Practice

Once you have written about it, and when you become comfortable enough, it would be good to talk your troubling situation over with a trusted friend, rabbi, priest, minister, mentor, or therapist. It's wonderful if you are lucky enough to have a true friend, one who totally accepts you as you are, and whom you can trust with your deepest secrets.

There are times you need to sort your thoughts before you can talk about them. There are times when you might feel upset or afraid and can't even put a finger on what's bothering you. Here are a few more ideas about journaling, just to help you get started on expressing yourself. You can finish one of the following sentences:

Today I feel _____.

Today I will _____.

I was really affected by _____.

When I think about (a person or incident) I feel _____

_____.

There are no rules about journaling. Actually, the only rules are what journaling *isn't*. We don't worry about spelling or punctuation or grammar. We're not concerned about neatness or handwriting. It is just for our own eyes. It is private. Remember, if you are concerned about someone seeing it, write in the front PERSONAL AND PRIVATE. READ AT YOUR OWN RISK.

It feels so good to express whatever
is bothering me on paper or to a trusted person.
God gives me all the courage I need to tell
someone what is bothering me.

Time for
Self-Compassion

"Compassion isn't some kind of
self-improvement project or ideal that
we're trying to live up to. Having compassion
starts and ends with having compassion
for all those unwanted parts of ourselves,
all those imperfections that we
don't even want to look at."

—*Pema Chödrön*

*A*hhh . . . self-compassion! What a blessing! It is so much
better than beating myself up as I used to do:

"You're not good enough."

"They're better than you."

"That was a stupid thing to say!"

"You only did five things out of the ten on your to-do
  list!"

This was the language I used on myself. And it made me
feel terrible. Self-compassion means that we accept ourselves
just as we are—the wonderful things about ourselves and
the not-so-wonderful; the things we are proud of and those
which we would rather not let people see. Self-acceptance is
being gentle with ourselves.

Now I say, "It's okay, Ruthie," instead of beating myself up,
and this makes me smile.

This doesn't mean we don't work on changing. It means
we are okay in this moment. We are doing or have done the
best we could do. And that is good enough. In fact, that's
pretty terrific!

This Week's Practice

Be mindful of how you talk to yourself this week. Just
notice the times you are hard on yourself, when you are critical and judgmental. It would be good to write them down
which helps to increase your awareness. Use your journal.

Be sure not to judge yourself for judging! Simply notice the times with gentleness and compassion.

Find a sweet name you can call yourself. (I use "Ruthie.") It helps to keep us gentle with ourselves. I know when I do this, not only do I smile, but I have a softer feeling within me.

> *I accept who I am with love and compassion.*
>
> *I am okay just the way I am.*
>
> *It feels so good to tell myself that I am okay just the way I am.*
>
> *It feels so good to practice speaking to myself with love and compassion.*
>
> *I no longer need the judge and the critic in my life.*

Time for Habits

"When you refrain from habitual thoughts
and behavior, the uncomfortable feelings will still
be there. They don't magically disappear.
Over the years, I've come to call resting with
the discomfort 'the detox period,' because
when you don't act on your habitual patterns, it's
like giving up an addiction. You're left with
the feelings you were trying to escape.
The practice is to make a wholehearted
relationship with that."

—*Pema Chödrön*

I don't drink alcohol anymore as I know I can't have only one. I don't smoke for the same reason. I don't play games on my computer, go to casinos, or local gambling joints because I know I will always try to beat my last score. When I was young my brother and I used to hit a tennis ball against a brick wall to see who could do it the most times without missing. I remember getting up to over five-hundred times! So my addictions and compulsions and obsessions began very early in life.

Unless I make a clear intention and mean it, I spend too much time looking at my email and the stock market. I had to take a good look at how my obsessions were blocking me from living, taking time from more important things in my life, and some, like smoking and drinking, were even killing me.

It's about withholding from immediate gratification. It's about withholding from things we do that are so habitual, things we do without thinking. It's about making more time in your life for living with joy and happiness.

Obviously there are good habits and there are bad habits. And obviously, bad habits are hard to break. With the use of the newest scientific findings, bad habits just might be easier to break than we thought.

Science has found that there are certain chemicals in our brain such as serotonin, endorphins, and dopamine, that, when triggered, bring us happiness. They regulate the pleasure center of the brain. At the most basic level, it regulates motivation—it sends signals to receptors in the brain saying, "This feels good!"

Gambling, drinking, drugging, eating, even a cup of coffee are just a few of the many things that can stimulate these chemicals, and we naturally want more and more to keep feeling good. We can be triggered just by seeing a cup of coffee or a bottle of wine advertised on television. Dopamine will be stimulated and we want more of this good feeling. That good feeling will unconsciously drive the motivation to indulge. It's a conditioned response.

Checking our email isn't a trigger, but when we get an email it might be. When we check our email and find nothing new we become disappointed. We wanted that "hit," so to speak. We wanted that high. So we look again and again to find it. And we form a new habit! The same is true of checking our Facebook pages or seeing if we have a text or telephone message. Seeking adventure can become habitual. Some people are no longer stimulated after waterskiing, for example, and try skydiving next. When they become accustomed to the things they have tried, they look for more and different excitement.

This is what addiction is all about. Our brains and our bodies get used to whatever it is that we are addicted to, and we crave more. We get high when we get it. We get depressed if we don't. Our brains have formed new neural pathways, deeper and deeper grooves each time we give in, and they expect more and more. Once we have developed these habits, it's hard to stop.

We can build new neural pathways to turn on our dopamine, serotonin, and endorphin in new ways. Our words can trigger the same chemicals that just seeing we have a text message does, so how we speak to ourselves is important. Author Charles Duhigg, in his book *The Power of Habit*, writes about the cue, the trigger and the reward. We see something like a Dunkin' Donuts ad. This is the cue that triggers a desire for a cup of coffee. When we want to give up coffee, we need to change this habit by anticipating a new reward. Maybe we will have an ice cream, or save the money for a trip. Gradually, new grooves form so that the new habit will become more natural than the old habit.

In *Man's Search for Meaning*, Viktor E. Frankl wrote, "Between stimulus and response, there is a space. In that space is our power to choose our response. In our response lies our growth and our freedom." Scientists also have proven that mindfulness lets us see the space between stimulus and response where we can make a decision to step back and not react. I remember doing this when I gave up coffee. With alcohol or drug addiction it can be much harder but we can "think through the drink," call our sponsor, and pray.

My friend Patrick Smith shared about Frankl's quote: "How to allow myself to find this space of which Frankl speaks? Finding my breath and observing it a few times is one way. Slowing down our habitual responses to life's activities, allows an opportunity to see what one is doing and to maybe even have a choice in how the activity is carried out. Habits, useful or not, are so easily formed, but not so easily released."

We're training our brain to make new neural pathways which will be triggered in the future, rather than the automatic responses we had in the past. And I have found that smiling and acknowledging to myself that I didn't give in, giving myself a pat on the back, sets off the feel-good chemical dopamine and it makes me feel good! My good feeling is my reward.

Forming new habits follows the same principle. Start in a small way. If you want your house to be less cluttered, for example, start with picking up for ten minutes each evening and build up. If you want to eat more vegetables, add one vegetable at a time. Remember what it said about forming a new habit in the affirmations week. It takes twenty-one days to form a new habit. New pathways are forming in your brain and they are getting deeper and deeper and more automatic with each passing day.

This Week's Practice

This week, let's practice looking at our habits that aren't good for us, and make a list of those that we perform automatically. Look especially at the ones that take us away from the life we really want, the person we choose to be. If you find any habit over time too difficult to give up, you might consider getting help with a good therapist. There are also more than fifty twelve-step programs for all types of addictions, beyond the obvious ones for alcohol, drugs, gambling, and overeating. There are actually twelve-step programs for too much emailing and even one for procrastinators!

Spend some time this week really watching yourself. Please don't think yourself bad or weak when you look at a habit that is not good for you. This is a time for awareness and not judging. Just notice it and feel good about yourself for being aware. Then you can take some necessary steps to change.

For example, can you go this week easily without drinking, smoking, gambling, drugging, or whatever habit you know isn't good for you?

Can you look at your email, Facebook page, texts, and phone messages less often, perhaps once in the morning, at noon, and after dinner? (Unless something is urgent or work is involved.) Is there anything else you tell yourself you will only do once or not at all, but find yourself doing more often?

Be mindful when you reach for any one of these things to avoid feelings you don't want to feel. It could be as simple as boredom or as painful as frightening memories. These habits are so automatic that we turn to them without even thinking about them. With awareness, we can practice pausing, be aware of the discomfort—and watch it pass.

Remember to replace the old habit with a new one and anticipate a new reward.

Reread the quote at the beginning of this chapter by Pema Chödrön. She tells us that giving up habits is like detoxing, like giving up an addiction. We'll have uncomfortable feelings because we want our habit to help us feel better. And we're used to doing it! It's important to not run away from these feelings but to accept them and be with them. In time, they will recede and finally disappear.

Remember, the more mindful you are, the more aware you will be, and the more clearly you will see the harmful effects that these habits have over you in your life.

There is a very effective practice to help us remember not to continue a habit that isn't good for us. Wear a rubber band around your wrist. It can be a particular color for this week's practice. Snap it when you find yourself beginning to act on a habit you want to give up. This works very well in helping you to be aware of your thoughts and feelings and when to stop!

Are there good habits you would like to do more of? Are there any good habits you would like to add to your life?

When you discover a habit that is not good for you, say to yourself something like:

It feels so good not to _____ *today!*

When you make a decision to create a new habit in your life, with power, passion, and a smile on your face, say to yourself something like:

I'm proud of myself as I develop new, positive, and healthy habits!

Check out the week on Time for Affirmations for more information.

Time for Action

"Talk doesn't cook rice."

—Chinese Proverb

The best intentions get us nowhere unless we act on them. The old saying "The road to hell is paved with good intentions" is so true. We can intend to be kind, considerate, caring people. We can intend to make a difference in the world. But, as it is written in the Bible in the Book of James: "If a brother or sister is naked or without food, and you say 'Depart in peace; be warmed and filled' but give them nothing for their body, what does it profit?" Without action, they go hungry.

Another form of inaction is procrastination. I can get into an avoidance mode sometimes. I might even appear to have ADHD (attention-deficit, hyperactivity disorder) when this happens. Sometimes when I need to begin a new project, pay bills, write an uncomfortable email, or make an uncomfortable call, I might put it off. Or I might pay bills instead of editing the book I am working on. I might get online and go from email to the stock market to Google to email and back to the stock market again and on and on.

I'll tell myself only ten more minutes and then ten more minutes and then ten more minutes. After thirty minutes have gone by, it might be too late to begin whatever I set out to do in the first place.

I have found that by telling myself to *stop*, breathe in and out three times, and spend just a few minutes doing what I have been avoiding, I begin to get into it and the avoidance is over. It's the same when I avoid a to-do list. When I make myself do just one thing, I feel good about myself and can move on.

Rereading the week on habits is helpful for taking action.

This Week's Practice

Be mindful of what you do to avoid something you might not like to do or are afraid to do. Would you like to be more of service but find yourself stuck, thinking you don't have enough time? This week make a list of what you find out about yourself in this area.

Then, when you find yourself procrastinating, practice *stop* or *shhhh* and then breathe in and out three times.

Spend just a few minutes doing what you have been avoiding. You can stop after a few minutes, or you might find that you are into it and keep going. Either way, you are breaking the habit of avoidance and it feels good! Make telephone calls. Check in with friends. Write that letter. Pay that bill. Make that amend. Remember the feel-good chemicals: they are triggered by taking that first action step!

Sometimes dreams or ideas feel overwhelming, even impossible. Take just one step to make it happen and the second step often becomes obvious and doable. They say that a journey of a thousand miles begins with a single step. On the other hand, there are times when the dream is not doable. But we will never know by not trying.

If it is service you would like to do and find yourself procrastinating, make a decision to add just one hour a week of service to your life. Then follow it up with action. Choose just one thing where you feel you can contribute to the good of another. You'll find that one hour isn't overwhelming. If it leads to more, fine. If it doesn't, one hour is more than you were doing before and you will feel better about yourself.

It feels so good to know that God is
helping me do what needs to be done today.
I have all the time and energy
I need to do God's will.

Time for Authenticity

"It takes courage to grow up and
become who you really are."

—*E. E. Cummings*

I remember the days when it was thought that women
should serve their husbands and the only jobs that were
appropriate for them were as teachers and secretaries. I was
at a meeting one time right at the beginning of the women's
liberation movement, and the chairperson asked for someone to take notes. As the only woman in the room, he looked
directly at me and while trembling inside, I shook my head
no. The same thing happened when he asked someone to

make coffee. Again I shook my head no. I actually wanted to hide under the table, feeling very conspicuous, and knowing I wasn't the most popular person in the room. I was still insecure at that time and was concerned that people wouldn't like me. To say no to what was expected of me was very difficult.

Women have grown a lot in that area since then, as have I. Yet, many still have difficulty speaking up for themselves and being their authentic selves. Obviously, the fear of being rejected or looking foolish exists for men as well as women. While this has changed in the last few generations, men are still often taught to be strong and not to show emotions. This fear can feel much stronger than what it takes to be who you are. And there are still some of us who don't even know who we really are. Columnist and author Anna Quindlen wrote, "The thing that is really hard and really amazing, is giving up on being perfect and beginning the work of becoming yourself." To be authentic, both men and women need to give up the image of who they think they *should* be and discover who they really *are*.

Researcher Brené Brown suggests that authenticity is not something we have or don't have; it's a practice. She writes, "It's a collection of choices we make every day. The choice to be real. The choice to be honest. The choice to let our true self be seen."

This Week's Practice

Why not take some time to examine your fears this week? What holds you back from speaking up and coming from your true self? What could you lose by being brave?

Ask yourself, *Do I still worry about . . .*

What I think they want me to be?
My fear of what they will think of me?
What I think they expect me to be?
Do I still have the story I made up about me?

And if you do, think about author Byron Katie's question, "Who would you be without your stories?"

Are you still a people-pleaser?
Do you still fear trusting yourself?
Are you afraid to just be yourself?
How would you feel if you accepted yourself just as you are?
How would you feel if you no longer cared what other people thought?

I am a strong person with courage and
integrity and I choose to live authentically,
openly, honestly, and fearlessly.

Time for Self-Approval

> "By choosing to be our most authentic
> and loving self, we leave a trail
> of magic wherever we go."
>
> —*Unknown Sage*

This week and last week are very similar but I have chosen to separate them because I think it is more helpful this way. Last week's practice, Time for Authenticity, is about accepting ourselves with all our imperfections and warts. It's about looking at where you are not perfect, and not necessarily trying to change, but to accept yourself just as you are.

Time for Self-Approval looks more deeply into whom we really are and the parts of ourselves we are afraid to show the world. The boy who would rather write poetry but goes out for the baseball team because he is afraid the kids will call him a sissy. The girl who would rather play baseball but instead hangs out with her friends at the mall because she is afraid her friends will call her a tomboy. Or the girl who doesn't try her hardest because she was told no man will marry her if she is too smart. These are the areas we want to look at, in other words, whom we really are if we could let go of the need for approval.

The first time I heard the term *approval addiction* was on a video by author Caroline McHugh and it set my mind off into a whirl of thoughts. I know I used to be concerned with what people thought of me, and I wondered if it was still true. As I questioned myself, it was very clear that I had been addicted to your approval—anyone's approval. For years as a young adult I hid my drinking. I was so afraid if anyone knew they certainly would think less of me and they would try to get me to do something about it. (As if they could until I was ready!) I was filled with shame.

And then getting sober and discovering I was attracted to women, discovering I was a lesbian. At first I couldn't accept this. I thought something was wrong with me. Gradually I did accept it and even approved of this in myself. But for years and years I thought "if they knew they wouldn't like me." When speaking about my partner, I referred to her as "my partner" rather than simply saying "her" or "she." I still needed people's approval; my own approval wasn't enough. I tested talking about it a bit, first telling this one and then that one and finally, getting more and more comfortable, I finally got over it and was just myself. What freedom!

We can call the need for approval or acceptance an addiction or a habit. It doesn't matter. This need became stuck in our brain the first time we heard someone, most likely a parent, say we are less than or we should be different. Our brain remembers every time we felt not good enough or different than. It formed a deeper and deeper groove. It's harder for our brain to remember the compliments, but the put-downs stay stuck and are easily triggered. Dr. Rick Hanson uses the words Teflon and Velcro to explain this. It was more important for our brain to remember negative, fearful thoughts thousands of years ago because they kept us alert and helped us survive. They stuck like Velcro. Positive thoughts, on the other hand, slipped away like sliding off Teflon. They were not necessary for our survival.

Sandy Bierig wrote, "To accept ourselves as we are means to value our imperfections as much as our perfections." As we begin to accept ourselves with all our imperfections and neediness, outside approval will mean less and less. The more

I say "It's okay, Ruthie. You're terrific just the way you are," I'm taking off the mask that I wore when I tried to be the person I thought you would like. Author Christopher Germer, PhD, tells us that a moment of self-compassion can change your entire day. A string of such moments can change the course of your *life*. It takes time to get over what people will think. It might even take the help of a therapist.

Read the week on self-compassion as well. There will be a great deal more ideas there. Are you ready to be free?

This Week's Practice

You can begin by going over last's week's questions. Once you feel you have answered them honestly, here are a few more:

Are there questions I just looked at that still make me uncomfortable?

Are there any aspects of me that I don't like?

Do I still feel shame about some parts of who I am?

As we sit in mindfulness practice and notice what is occurring, without judging or evaluating, we begin to loosen the ties they hold on us.

Again, journaling is an excellent way to explore your truth, and to release it. Then, whenever you feel ready, talk to someone whom you know will accept you as you are without any judgment. And use the affirmations!

Try these affirmations. They can be very healing.

> *It feels so good to treat myself gently with love and compassion.*
>
> *I'm terrific just the way I am!*
>
> *I like myself today.*
>
> *I accept who I am today and feel good about myself.*
>
> *I accept myself just as I am!*

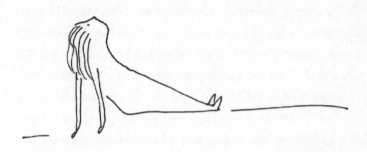

Time for Stillness

"It is through stillness, through the
reaching of an inner quiet, that one can get
the clarity that allows for the richest thinking.
Stillness involves daily discipline in order to
be developed. It is truly illuminating."

—*Anne Alexander Vincent,*
The Way to Stillness

Stillness. Just seeing the word brings me peace. I feel each
breath become longer. I'm aware of my chest rising and
falling. I slow down. My body feels softer. I feel this way when
I am mindful of where I am, what I am doing, and when I

am in deep conversation with someone. I feel this way when I meditate. I feel this way in nature, when I look closely at a flower, when I am at the beach, when I sit by any body of water. I feel this way when I stroke my cat's head when she is lying between my feet with her head on my ankle, when I am doing my inspirational morning readings right before I meditate.

I can create this feeling just by watching my breath as I breathe in and out three times. I can create this feeling at will when I remember to do it. And so can you! No matter what is going on in your life, no matter how stressed or anxious you might feel, practice being still. Stillness brings us closer to the God of our understanding. It connects us with our inner spirit, our true self.

Stillness offers us silence, that inner quiet Anne wrote about, if we choose to experience it. Or we can decide to think deeply, to investigate a situation that might be concerning us, or contemplate a line from a poem or philosophical writing, or we can simply be silent with our thoughts, and be filled with peace and joy.

This Week's Practice

Take some time each day to be still. Maybe you have a special place in your house or outside where you can go. Maybe just closing the door in your office will accomplish this for you.

You might want to create a shrine, a sacred place that has special objects that have heartfelt meanings for you. I used to think the word was associated with religions but it doesn't have to be. I have a bookcase next to my side of our bed where I have spiritual books. On the top I have a beautifully carved Quan Yin, the Goddess of Compassion, a special gift from my friend Diane to celebrate my ordination into Thich Nhat Hanh's Order of Interbeing. There is also my God box, a candle, and a few other meaningful items. I always feel the stillness when I am aware of my shrine, when I stop and take the time to look at each item.

Nature is always a wonderful place to practice stillness. I'm personally drawn to water, whether it is the ocean, lake, river, pond, or stream. Now that I am living on the west coast of Florida, I am so grateful to be at the beach more often. Water has a special effect on me and immediately acts like a tranquilizer.

For some people it is the mountains or the desert or their own backyard. Simply sit.

Be still.

And watch your life change.

It is extraordinarily peaceful to take time
each day to be still. In this stillness I
feel a close connection to God.

time for investigation!

Time for Investigation

"For the wise have always known
that no one can make much of his life until
self-searching has become a regular habit,
until he is able to admit and accept what he finds,
and until he patiently and persistently tries
to correct what is wrong."

—*Bill W., Cofounder of Alcoholics Anonymous*

Now that we are more familiar with stillness, it is easier to listen to our mind. How many times a day do you listen to and believe your mind? I have read that the average adult has 40,000 to 60,000 thoughts a day and whether this figure is true or not, we certainly have many thousands of thoughts. And many are negative, causing us suffering. The good news is that we can change them! We have to, because our thoughts create our feelings and if we don't change them, we are going to be walking around angry, fearful, negative, full of self-pity, or any one of the many more negative feelings that pull us down.

"I'll never make it."

"I'm not as good as . . ."

"I have too much to do."

What's important to know is that thoughts are not facts. As one of my meditation teachers, Fred Eppsteiner, says, "As long as we listen to our mind, we are lost and we will never change." Once you begin questioning your thoughts, you will be amazed at how your life changes. But we have to look deeply.

Very often, what we think and feel and react to in the present moment is influenced by our past experiences, or our perceptions of our past experiences, and our thoughts about our past experiences. For example, if I see a man who reminds me of my father and I have unhealed, fearful memories of my father, I might feel fear without even knowing this new person. Or I might feel fear if I have to go to the dentist because I had a painful experience with a dentist in the past.

I have practiced a few powerful and revealing exercises which have been a great help to me. One is suggested by Byron Katie who learned, after years of deep depression, that all our suffering comes from believing our stressful thoughts are true. If we question our thoughts, we don't suffer. She suggests we ask four questions when we have a negative thought about ourselves:

1. Is it true?
2. Can I absolutely know that it's true?
3. How do I react, what happens when I believe that thought?
4. Who would I be without the thought?

She found this true of everyone. "Freedom is as simple as that. I found that suffering is optional. I found a joy within me that has never disappeared, not for a single moment. That joy is in everyone, always."

Another question we can ask ourselves comes from a Buddhist practice taught to me by meditation teacher Joanne Friday. Writing in my book *Wrinkles Don't Hurt: The Joy of Aging Mindfully,* she taught me to ask "Are you sure?" When she was diagnosed with cancer, her immediate reaction was fear that she was going to die. She stopped and asked herself "Are you sure?" and knowing that she wasn't sure, she chose "not to waste any of my remaining moments in fear and speculation."

Joanne also taught me to look deeply when I have unpleasant feelings to discover when I felt this way earlier in my life. Then, look deeper again until I reach the first time I felt them. Once I found the source, I could begin to heal.

Investigating in this way has helped me live more fearlessly and joyfully in the present moment.

This Week's Practice

"Listen with the ear of your heart," wrote St. Benedict. This is so important. Be gentle and non-judgmental with yourself as you investigate. Be self-compassionate.

Try this for yourself this week. Each time you have a feeling that is unpleasant, such as fear, self-pity, or anger, be mindful of it. If you have time at that moment to stop and investigate, do so. Ask yourself if it's true or if you are sure. You can also look deeply to find the source.

If you are too busy, you can make a note of the feelings and explore them when you have more time. You will be amazed how these simple questions will reveal the truth and help you experience the peace of the present moment.

Do the same with the stories that go round and round in your mind. We tell ourselves so many stories and we believe them! For example, we might hear, "He did this and it completely ruined my day!" And this same story can replay over and over again until we stop it. Take some time to listen to your stories and ask yourself, *Is this true? Can I absolutely know that it's true? How do I react, what happens when I believe that thought? Who would I be without the thought?* And, finally, *Am I sure?* And begin letting these stories go!

Be aware of your thoughts. Be mindful. Know that many of your thoughts and all of your stories are simply your perceptions of how you see a situation. They are usually far from the truth. As soon you do notice the negative thought, say to yourself, whether you believe it or not, *I'm terrific just the way I am.* Or if this sounds too unreal, say, *I'm okay just the way I am,* or, *Everything is flowing easily and effortlessly.* It might help to write down your stories and your negative thoughts in your journal when you discover them. Writing things down helps us to remember them and be more aware when they come up next time. Writing them down also helps you see that they are not true.

It feels so good to know that I no longer
have to believe my thoughts. I can find peace
in asking if they are true and am I sure.

Time for Contemplation

"As your mind grows quieter
and more spacious, you can begin to
see self-defeating thought patterns for what
they are, and open up to other,
more positive options."

—*Sharon Salzberg*

Once we have established some stillness and silence in our lives, we can take time for contemplation. Once we have quieted our minds, stopped our worrying and our thoughts about the past and the future, some of the big questions we might have wondered about over the years can be investigated.

These are the types of questions we cannot even touch when our minds are busy. Deep questions such as who am I, and is there a purpose in my life? Is there a power greater than myself? Does God exist?

Some of us are fortunate to have found these answers in our lives. Many others still wonder, still don't know. Thich Nhat Hanh tells us that we cannot discover these answers until we silence our minds. He writes that when you have silence within, "You can find some answers to these questions and hear the deepest call of your hearts . . . Mindfulness gives you the inner space and quietness that allow you to look deeply, to find out who you are and what you want to do with your life."

For me there came a time in my life when I simply knew, when I finally found the path I had been searching for, the path that deep in my heart I knew was there but had no idea where or what it was. It came from prayer and meditation and experiencing, living what I was hearing. And over time there was a deep knowing, which gives me great peace and joy every day.

This Week's Practice

When you have a block of time, sit quietly. Breathe in and out softly. Sit mindfully until you become aware that your mind is quiet. Contemplate these deep questions:

Who am I really?

What do I deeply long for?

Why am I here?

What parts of me do I still hide?

What are my fears?

Why do I still suffer?

Is there anyone I need to forgive?

What am I holding on to that blocks me from feeling joy?

What is my purpose?

Am I living my purpose?

Make a commitment to sit with these or other questions each day this week. I hope you can make this a regular habit in your life. Even when you think you have the answers, there will always be more to learn. You might not receive answers immediately. You might not even be sure that you think the answers are the truth. You might hear some things that you

want to try out or discuss with others. But in time, when the
time is right, you will know. And you will feel joy.

> *It feels so good to know*
> *that there is always more to learn.*
> *Exploring the truth is part*
> *of my spiritual path.*

Time for Releasing

> "Sometimes you don't realize the
> weight of something you've been carrying
> until you feel the weight of its release."
>
> —*Unknown Sage*

Now that we have spent a week on contemplation, there might be things that came up that are disturbing. Unanswered questions. Unfinished business. People we need to forgive. It's important that we find a way to release them. We cannot be free until we do.

Imagine a kettle boiling on the stove, the whistling getting stronger and stronger to let us know it is ready. As the steam built up in the kettle, there is no longer any room for it in the kettle and it must be released. If there is no place for it to escape, the cover would finally burst from the kettle, and could cause harm.

This is the same with all human beings. If we are carrying with us negativity, regret, and anger we have to find a way to release it or we, too, will burst. We will either shut down, become depressed, explode in anger, or we will eventually get physically sick.

We have to express our feelings in some way, whether by talking it over with a friend, advisor or professional, and if this is too hard at first, as I wrote before, we can journal about it. This will help release some of the emotion around the pain and then we will be more ready to talk it over with someone we trust.

Acceptance comes next. Accept the situation and let it go. Prayer and meditation help. This does not mean that we will get immediate relief. Sometimes answers come when you least expect them. There was a woman whom I saw at a weekly meeting I attended. Something about her simply annoyed me. I did everything I knew how to do to let go of this feeling, to accept her as she was. I looked at myself to see if I had the same characteristics that annoyed me about her. I sent her *metta* (prayers and thoughts for her well-being and happiness): May you be happy. May you be peaceful. May you be free from suffering. I prayed for her. I prayed that these feelings about her would be removed. I talked about it to a friend in an attempt to release it. Nothing helped. Week after week the same irritation rose inside of me. Then I had an "aha!" moment. I read something in Janet Conner's book, *Soul Vows,* that made me stop. I felt my breath slow down. I let this truth sink in. I knew I had my answer. Janet wrote: "God loves _____ as much as God loves me." I smiled and nodded my head in agreement. It was over.

This can be a wonderfully freeing, opening week for you.

Spring Blessing

One day you wake up
able to name the weight
you've been carrying.
Realizing it's not part of your body or your being,
not essential in any way to journeying or joy,
you set it down gently, without fanfare
in the long soft grass at the side of the road
and walk on
surprised to find yourself
smiling in the warm sun
for no particular reason.

—Oriah Mountain Dreamer © 2015

This Week's Practice

Take some time this week to be aware of your messages from the past. As you go about your week, listen to those voices in your head that are keeping you stuck from moving on, from being open, from feeling your joy. See what feelings are triggered by these thoughts. Also be aware of when your buttons are being pushed that lead to these thoughts. Perhaps by something said to you, or a situation in a book you are reading, or a TV story or movie you are watching.

Here are some of the ways we know we're holding on. When we hear ourselves say, in our thoughts or out loud:

"I wish I would have . . ."

"I wish I hadn't . . ."

And the extreme, "I'll never be able to forgive myself for . . ."

Or "I'll never be able to forgive _____ for . . ."

Journaling helps you to get in touch with these thoughts and others like them. One good exercise is to write down each of the above sentences and finish them. It will help to refer to the week on journaling for more information. And as you have read before, talking about whatever is on your mind is a great release.

Another wonderfully helpful way to let go is to create a "God bag" or "God box." I've used them for years and have found almost instant relief in them. Simply take any bag or box and write the words "God" or "Higher Power" or whatever name you give to a power greater than yourself on it. Whenever you have a situation you don't know how to handle, a characteristic that is creating suffering in you or someone else, you can find peace by turning it over to a power greater than yourself. Simply write it down and put it in the God bag or box. This is a physical act of turning it over, of letting the situation go. Then, every time you worry about it, know that you have turned it over. There is tremendous relief in this.

Another fun way to turn things over is to get a used can. Wash it out and take off any labeling. Then write "GOD CAN" on it. Write down what you want to turn over and put it in the can. Then say, "I can't. God can!" It's bound to make you feel lighter, no matter how serious the problem is, and you might even smile.

I am so grateful God gives me all
the willingness, courage, and insight I need
to look deeply and let go of all that is holding
me back from being free of my past.

Time for Optimism

"If you accept the expectations of
others, especially negative ones, then you
never will change the outcome."

—*Michael Jordan*

Some people are born with a propensity for optimism, while others tend toward pessimism. Studies show that our personalities are based 50 percent on our genes, 10 percent on our circumstances, and 40 percent on our intentional activity. Remember, in the neuroplasticity week we learned that our brains are not hardwired. Up until now most of us have used our brains in ways that created inflexible behaviors.

As you have already read, scientists have now proven that we have the ability to rewire and create new neural circuits at any age! The other part of this exciting news is that our thoughts can rewire our brain.

I was very fortunate to have parents who encouraged me. My mother always encouraged my ideas and my father often told the story of how, when he took me skiing, I would fall and pick myself up over and over again. He would say to anyone who would listen, "Ruth can do anything." And for a long time I believed him! This led me to have a very strong inclination toward optimism.

Sandy Bierig writes, "Every time someone starts a new company or writes a book or a song or buys a house or decides to go to school or get married or do anything else that expresses their belief in themselves or others, optimism is born, a chance is taken, a life realized. We would not have electricity in our homes or cars or airplanes or any number of conveniences born of hope if people had not taken a chance."

In spite of seemingly overwhelming odds, some people have refused to allow those odds to stop them from reaching out to experience their dreams. For instance, the brothers that started the "Life is good" T-shirt company began with only $78, an old van, and their dreams. Today, they have many products for sale and many outlets for items that, I think, make people smile and feel optimistic about themselves, and joyously wear messages for all to see and take to heart. Their company mission is to spread optimism. I have four "Life is good" T-shirts!

The owner of the gym I attend told me she had sold the gym. She was looking forward to taking some time off, doing some things around the house, and moving on to her next adventure. I suggested she write the affirmation, "God gives me all the courage I need to find my next adventure." She smiled and answered that she didn't need to write it—she totally believes it.

This Week's Practice

Many of the weeks that you have practiced thus far in this book can help you be more optimistic. You can look over the weeks again for meditation, prayer, mindfulness, morning, intention, neuroplasticity, and purpose, just to name a few.

Journaling also helps. Take some time to be aware of whether your thoughts are optimistic or pessimistic, and investigate them through your journaling. Ask yourself what messages you heard while you were growing up and whether you still believe them. Look at the times when you took chances, or when you held back because of fear or lack of belief in yourself.

Think about one thing you would have liked to do but never had the courage to do it. Take a chance. Go for it! If you fail it's okay. As Sandy Bierig wrote, "We would not have electricity in our homes or cars or airplanes or any number of conveniences born of hope if people had not taken a chance."

Today I know I'm being
guided by a power greater than myself.
I look forward to the unknown around the
next bend in the road, the adventure over the next hill.
I know my Higher Power gives me all the strength
that I need as I dare to take one new step
at a time toward a new challenge.

Time for Reviewing

"At any moment, you have a choice,
that either leads you closer to your spirit
or further away from it."

—*Thich Nhat Hanh*

This is one of my very favorite weeks. It summarizes all the positive messages we learned so far. You can spend one week concentrating on being mindful of the words that cause our suffering and how we can turn them into joy.

For example, when we become mindful that our thoughts are focused on "I'm not good enough," we can stop, breathe in and out three times, and say, "I'm terrific just the way I am!" Or if this feels too impossible, say, "I am okay just the way I am."

Another very simple step in stopping obsessive thinking is breathing. As we develop the regular habit of mindfulness, we become aware of our obsessive thoughts more quickly. As soon as you notice one, *stop* and be aware as you *breathe* in and out three times. You'll find by the third breath the worry thought will have disappeared.

When we become aware of our thoughts concerning a health issue, we can *stop, breathe* in and out three times, and say, "I'm not going there. I don't know anything yet. Everything is okay in this moment."

It is very important not to believe our thoughts! Meditation teacher Bill Menza tells us "We have about 60,000 thoughts a day. Many are repetitious. Where they come from or go is a mystery. But we do know that they are not real. You can't put a thought on an examination table. They are just creations of our mind. . . . If you follow these suggestions you will find more and more that your negative thoughts have been replaced with positive ones so you are more calm and peaceful. Also, that you are more directly experiencing the many wonders and miracles all around you."

So read and reread your This Week's Practice pages and *practice*! The more you do this the more you will have joy and peace in your life.

This Week's Practice

Here are some of the "turn-around" thoughts that have been suggested so far in your readings. As you grow in your ability to bring awareness to the thoughts that influence your feelings, you will be able to shift to them more quickly. Negative, fearful, jealous, judgmental thoughts will continue to come up for you because they are part of your habit energy. Just remember not to judge them. It's the *second* thought that counts. When you become aware of them, turn them around and change them.

Is this how I want to feel?

Is it true?

Am I sure?

How would I feel if I didn't think this way? What would I do differently if I didn't think this way?

What if I were open and let go of my preconceived ideas?

What if I didn't care what anyone thought of me?

How would I feel if I were willing to forgive _____?

How would I feel if I were willing to let go of my obsessive thinking?

These are some questions you can explore. As you begin to get used to this process, you'll probably come up with some more of your own that will be helpful.

Select a few turn-arounds that speak strongly to you and put them on sticky notes where you can see them. One thing about sticky notes is that there is some point when you are so used to them, you no longer see them. They blend into the background. I once read that this happens in, I think, eight days. So move them often! Write in different colors so they will stand out for you. Keep doing this until it all becomes a habit.

It feels so good to know that I can feel good
simply by changing my thoughts.

Time for Evaluation

"A truthful evaluation of yourself gives
feedback for growth and success."

—*Brenda Johnson Padgitt*

This marks six months, the halfway point, of *Time for Me*. If you have gone in order, you've been practicing the suggestions you read for twenty-six weeks. It's perfectly okay if you have taken more time on some of the weeks. This is a good time to stop and to evaluate how you are doing, and whether you are noticing any significant changes in your life. If you have been serious and really taken a week or more to practice each suggestion, you probably noticed changes in you and your life as the weeks passed. On the other hand, if you have simply skimmed the book or did a week here or there, you'll obviously have fewer, if any changes. It's often difficult to see changes on a day-to-day basis. If you look back to six months or to where you were a year ago, it will be clearer for you.

Take some time in the weekly practice page to answer the questions you'll find there and, depending on your answers, you might want to go back to the beginning of this book and start over or concentrate on some specific weeks again.

Time for Me is meant for you to go at your own pace. Please don't judge yourself, no matter what you find. You can always go back and begin again or pick the book up at another time.

This Week's Practice

Have I noticed any changes in myself?

Am I happier . . . more peaceful . . . compassionate . . . more generous . . . relaxed . . . patient?

Do I meditate daily?

Am I more mindful?

Are my relationships better?

Have I gained any insights into myself?

Have I been able to let go of some of my blocks?

Do I suffer less?

Am I less angry . . . depressed . . . sad . . . judgmental?

Have people noticed a difference in me?

Am I more purposeful or does my life have more
  meaning?

Am I more open?

Do I feel freer?

> *It's exciting to know I can become*
> *happier, freer, and more full of purpose, just*
> *by taking time this week to practice*
> *what I am learning.*

Time for Purpose

"It is only when we truly
know and understand that we have
a limited time on earth—and that we have
no way of knowing when our time is up—
that we will begin to live each day to
the fullest, as if it was the
only one we had."

—Elisabeth Kübler-Ross

We have practiced stillness and contemplation. We can come to know our heart's purpose in our life for now. What we discover for today might not be true for tomorrow.

Life is impermanent. Everything changes. Purposes are born within us and can fade away, only to come back to us in a new form.

Carl Jung described maturity as an awakening to the need to live a life of spiritual purpose, rather than simply fulfilling the basic needs of physical survival or pursuing pleasure. I felt very deeply that I had a purpose in my life in addition to being a wife, mother, daughter, and friend, but I never knew what it was. I was not mature enough to discover it until I began my journey into my recovery from alcoholism. First, once I got sober I knew I had something to share with others. This filled me with great joy. Then my purpose became very clear and it led to starting a halfway house for recovering alcoholic women with my partner Sandy. I used to sit on the shore of a lovely pond close to where I was working and pray very hard, begging God to let me know what was next, what was I supposed to do tomorrow, next week, five years from then? When the halfway house was barely complete we started a three-quarter house, and then a job-training program, and opened four stores. On and on. Never satisfied with where we were but always needing to know what to do next. I was finally helping people and I was loving it!

Gradually, over the years, I let go of some of the need to know and began simply praying for the knowledge of God's will for me and the power to carry that out. And finally, I no longer had the need to know. I trusted I would know when I needed to know, on a daily basis.

I was standing outside the women's prison at Massachusetts Correctional Institution (MCI) Framingham one day many years ago. Sandy had started one of the first addictions programs in the country for inmates there and I had just finished teaching meditation. I knew I was helping thirty or so women in the prison and eighteen women in the halfway house. I felt I should be doing more. I remember looking up and asking God what I should do next. I received an immediate answer. I didn't hear the answer, I just became conscious of the answer. I knew the answer with all my heart: "Write a book!" This soon became *The Journey Within: A Spiritual Path to Recovery*, the beginning of many books.

The Eleventh Step prayer of the Twelve Steps of Recovery of Alcoholics Anonymous puts it very well: "Sought through prayer and meditation to improve our conscious contact with God, seeking only for the knowledge of God's will for us and the power to carry that out." I say this every morning.

Every morning the Dalai Lama says, "I dedicate all my actions of this day to the benefit of all living beings." I try to remember to add this to my daily prayers.

Our purposes change over the years. At one time it might mean we are to go to college, or to learn a trade. Parenting might be a full-time job for many years. Some people think their purpose is to make money, to become rich, to have the things that will make them happy. Those are purposes based on ego. Here we are talking about a spiritual purpose, a purpose greater than ourselves. Somewhere deep within you, you will know when it is time to do something new.

Philosopher Dr. Howard Thurman said, "Don't ask yourself what the world needs. Ask yourself what makes you come alive and then go and do that. Because what the world needs is people who have come alive."

There is another way to look at our purpose; as smaller purposes that are pieces of our larger ones. Our daily purpose. We can find purpose in everything we are doing. If we are washing the dishes, that is our purpose in that moment. If we are taking a shower, going to work, planting seeds or pulling weeds, smiling at a stranger, helping a friend, these are our purposes in these moments. Some are mundane but our lives consist of many small, mundane moments. Some are filled with things that need to be done. Some are simply moments of living. If we are thinking these moments are unimportant, and we are waiting to get at our "bigger, true purpose," we will be missing our opportunity for joy in everyday life.

Author and scholar Dr. Jean Houston says it's not too late to start living your life's purpose.

This Week's Practice

So many people over the ages have explained, far better than I can, the value of service. Read them each morning. Let these thoughts inspire you.

"The purpose of life is a life of purpose."

—*George Bernard Shaw*

"Generosity brings happiness to
every stage of its expression. We experience
joy at forming the intention to be generous.
We experience joy at the very act of giving
something. And we experience joy in
remembering the fact that we have given."

—*The Buddha*

"Among the many aspects of life
that give us meaning, helping others is
one of the most rewarding."

—*Carolyn Myss*

"To this day I believe we are here on earth to live,
grow, and do what we can to make this world a
better place for all people to enjoy freedom."

—*Rosa Parks*

"All men are responsible for each other."

—*The Talmud*

"I shall pass through this world but once.
Any good therefore that I can do or any kindness
that I can show to any human being,
let me do it now. Let me not defer or neglect it,
for I shall not pass this way again"

—*Stephen Grellet*

"Service to others has helped me to
grow in many ways. It has taught me patience,
compassion, and understanding. It has broadened
and enriched my outlook on life."

—*Joann Malone*

"There is no purpose for your life
greater than to recognize your own beauty,
power, and worth, and to share it."

—*Alan Cohen*

Some say we're supposed to be happy and therefore do
things that make us happy. Others say we find happiness by
helping others. The truth is we have to find our truth for
ourselves.

This week ask yourself: *Is my life fulfilling? Satisfying? Am I happy? What expands my aliveness?*

Make a list of all things you enjoy. Provide the most service to the most people by expanding your aliveness to those around you. What would you do if you knew you were going to die one year from today? How do you want to be remembered?

Many years ago I wrote a little book titled, *Make Your Heart Sing*. In it I asked:

What makes your heart sing?

What brings meaning to your life?

What fills you with joy?

Ask yourself these questions this week. Spend some time quietly journaling your answers.

There is a wonderful exercise that I found brings me answers that are least expected. With your dominant hand write this question to the God of your understanding, "What is my purpose for this time of my life?"

And with your opposite hand, your non-dominant hand, write the answer that comes to you. You will find that this process will slow you down and bring you into the right side of your brain where we find our intuition, our inner knowing. You will be amazed at what will be revealed!

"Might love be at the heart of every question that has to do with the meaning of a particular life or a special moment?" asks psychiatrist and author Jean Shinoda Bolen. She adds that we must know ourselves and what matters to us in order to choose wisely.

It feels so good to know that
God lets me know my purpose for each
day and gives me the power
to carry that out.

I have a purpose today.
As I let go and let God, this purpose
is becoming more and more clear.
My heart is full of joy and love as I move
more toward God's will for me.

Time for Fun

I know I have a tendency to be serious. I usually have a
lot to do and make an effort not to work on weekends.
My idea of fun is spending a morning of the weekend at the
beach with my partner when the weather is good, and watching a Red Sox game during the baseball season (even when
they are having a bad year!). Gardening, bridge, poker, and
some board games are also on the top of my fun list. Actually,
I enjoy a lot of the times when I write. And although I don't
let people hear me, I love to sing when I am alone.

Kathi, a good friend of mine from Cape Cod, sent me the
following she has been having some fun with:

"Here's something I have been doing that is silly and fun. I collected some pretty rocks—about twelve or thirteen at the beach—some round, some flat, but interesting to me. They were sitting on my bureau, minding their own business . . . when I decided to make little stacks, little stonehenges or towers. Sometimes they fall over when I walk into the room so I make new combinations.

"It is very silly but such fun to see these little creations when I walk into the room! (It takes concentration and discipline, a steady hand, and an appreciation of impermanence while making the tower.)"

This Week's Practice

This week think about what's on your fun list. Do you have one? If not, why not make one? You can save one day for fun or, if you're too busy for that, at least a morning or a few hours. It will be something you will look forward to beforehand and remember afterwards, and those thoughts will bring you good feelings in addition to the actual fun time you take.

Be sure to do at least one thing this week that is on your fun list—more if you have time.

I'm making time this week to do something just for fun.

Time for Kindness

"Be kind whenever possible.
It is always possible."

—*Tenzin Gyatso, 14th Dalai Lama*

How do you want to be treated? With respect? With kindness? With understanding? With love? Don't answer quickly; take some time to think about it. Think about how you feel when you are treated with kindness. Now think how you feel when you are treated unkindly. Now you know how someone else will feel when you treat them one way or the other way. Author and motivational speaker Zig Ziglar had a thought about kindness and generosity that made me smile. He said, "Among the things you can give and still keep are your word, a smile, and a grateful heart."

Many years ago my son Bob wrote the following two lines which I think are very profound: "The more I work with people and the more I go through life, the more I realize that people just want to be happy. If I take five minutes out of each day to remember to treat people the same way I want to be treated, we can accomplish wonderful things together." He was very wise!

I had a wonderful lesson one day at the gym. After I did all but one of my exercises, I saw a man sitting on the bench of the machine I wanted to use. After waiting a few minutes, I asked him if he was going to use that machine. He said he was stretching and he would be done soon. After a few more minutes I asked if he could stretch somewhere else so I could use the machine.

He said no.

I said, a bit sarcastically, "Thanks! Have a great day!"

I had to leave as my time had run out and I walked angrily to the car. I could feel the resentment in me and I said to myself, *Is this how you want to feel?*, the question that has been helping me considerably. I knew the answer was *no*!

And I remembered phrases such as, "Every being is an abode of God, worthy of respect and reverence." (a Hindu scripture), and, "Be kind to unkind people. They need it the most."

Amazing how quickly my feelings changed!

This Week's Practice

Take time this week to be aware of how you treat others. Notice how you speak to them when you are in a good mood or in a not-so-good mood, when you are impatient, when you don't get what you want, when you are waiting for someone who is late.

Practice pausing before you answer quickly when you are upset so you can have the space to calm down. You could take a walk outside if you're really angry. You'll find that this one week can help you create new habits, which can improve your relationship with others.

There is a great website called *www.kindspring.org*. Its purpose is to pass on ideas on how to be kind. A few of their suggestions are:

Frame an inspiring quote and give it to a friend.

Pay the toll for the car behind you.

Give a parking spot to another car.
Add your own here.

*I'm building a lifetime practice
of kindness.*

Time for Metta

"So watch the thought and its ways with care,
and let it spring from love, born out
of concern for all beings."

—*The Buddha*

Metta loving-kindness is a wonderful Buddhist practice. The word *metta* is a Pali word with two root meanings. One is *gentle* and the other is *friend*. We can use it to bring love to ourselves and those we love. We can use it to let go of negative feelings toward people we are having difficulty with, and we can use it to send the energy of peace and love to individuals and out into the world.

It is said that we really can't love others until we love ourselves. If we are blocked in any way from self-love, this same
block will be a barrier in our love for someone else. Therefore, sending metta to ourselves is a wonderful step in feeling
good about ourselves. When we are willing to send love to
someone who has harmed us, we are released from the blocks
of our anger and resentments. This is a wonderful exercise
to use when we want to forgive someone, to find freedom
from our resentments, for ending our personal suffering, and
ending the suffering of others. Author and Buddhism teacher
Jack Kornfield tells us, "The quality of loving kindness is the
fertile soil out of which an integrated spiritual life can grow."

I have used this when someone I know is suffering. And
I have used this when I am angry at someone. Within a few
days the anger disappears. This has worked every time for
me. It's difficult to stay angry at someone when we are willing
to send love and peace to that person.

The Buddha said that the intimacy and caring that fills
our hearts as the force of loving-kindness develops will bring
advantages. Some of these are: we will sleep easily, we will
wake easily, we will have pleasant dreams, people will love us,
our face will be radiant, and our mind will be serene.

My friend Joann Malone wrote, "Prayer is part of my daily
mindfulness meditation practice today. In meditation I often
hold suffering people in my family, community, or in war

zones in my heart, in the circle of friends meditating together. I send 'metta' or loving-kindness to them, asking the Universe that they be safe, happy, and free of suffering."

This Week's Practice

Either during or after your morning meditation, or any time during the day, practice metta. Find time each day this week to make it a part of your week. Here is a long version and a short version.

Metta Practice for When You Have Time

Begin by taking a few minutes to be with your breath, breathing in peace and breathing out tension. When you feel calm and relaxed, imagine that you are in your inner sanctuary. This is the place where your heart lives, a place where you feel love. Say to yourself:

May I be happy . . . May I be peaceful . . . May I be free from suffering.

Now bring someone into your heart whom you care about and say:

May you be happy . . . May you be peaceful . . . May you be free from suffering.

Next bring in a neutral person, perhaps a neighbor you barely know or someone in the local community and say:

May you be happy . . . May you be peaceful . . . May you be free from suffering.

Now if you want to, bring in someone you would like to forgive or receive forgiveness from, someone whom you would like to come to peace with, and say:

May you be happy . . . May you be peaceful . . . May you be free from suffering.

Expand that feeling and send these thoughts of loving-kindness to everyone you know, your family, friends, and colleagues.

Now extend that feeling to people with life-threatening diseases, to the addicts and the alcoholics who need treatment, the hungry and the homeless, the people in wars or living with threat of war or the result of war, and to our leaders who think war is an answer to peace, and say:

As we want to be happy, may everyone be happy. As we want to be peaceful, may everyone be peaceful. And as we want to be free from suffering, may everyone be free from suffering.

You can repeat these phrases over and over for as long as you like. Take some time to let *yourself* feel filled with the love you have brought to yourself and others.

There are many variations of metta. Create your own phrases. For example, if you notice you are impatient, you might want to say, "May I be filled with patience." If you are having a difficult time with yourself, you can concentrate on bringing love into your own heart and say, "May I be filled with love." If you are angry at someone, you might say, "May I be free from resentments."

Metta Practice for When You Have Only a Moment or Two

Begin with yourself. Breathe into your heart where you feel love. Say to yourself:

> May I be happy . . .
>> May I be peaceful . . .
>>> May I be free from suffering.

You can either stop here until you feel better about yourself, or repeat this for someone you love, someone who might be suffering, or someone with whom you are having difficulty. You can send it out into the universe to add peaceful and loving energy to the world.

This is a wonderful exercise that you can practice in solitude for what is going on in your life at any particular time.

*Today I am bringing love and peace into
my heart and sending it out to others.*

Time for Forgiveness

"As hard as forgiveness might be at times,
it is a gift we give ourselves.
This includes, by the way, forgiving the
most important person—yourself!"

—*Unknown Sage*

How can we possibly forgive the person at whom we are so angry? I felt this way about my father for years. Look what he did to me! After all, I didn't do anything wrong!

As I learned to look within, to be honest, to see what my thoughts did to my feelings, I realized that my anger was causing me harm. When I became honest with myself I could certainly see what anger did to me, not the other person. It made me miserable. It made me tense. I could feel it in my clenched jaw and fists. My breath was shallow. While I stayed angry and held on to my self-righteous thoughts, I could not find joy or happiness. Thich Nhat Hanh compares anger to a hot coal. It's like having a hot coal in our hand, ready to throw it at someone. Obviously, it's only burning us.

I learned to ask myself, *Is this how I want to feel?* I learned to pray for the other person, to accept the other person as they were, knowing they were that way because of causes and conditions in their past. I did not have to be friends with them. I didn't even have to like them. I just had to let the anger go. Carolyn Myss wrote, "Forgiveness, quite frankly, is the most selfish thing you can do. Because it is the greatest thing you can do for yourself."

I tried many things to let go of my anger toward my father. It actually took years of praying for it to finally end. My father loved baseball and when I was young he took me to many games. He died years before the Red Sox won their first World Series in more than eighty years. That year an unexpected thought suddenly came to me, *My father would have loved to see this!* I suddenly became filled with an overwhelming love for my father, and a deep gratitude for all he had given me, from teaching me how to swim, to taking me skiing, to teaching me to love all sports. It was a complete turn-around. It was so profound I was able to dedicate my book, *Wrinkles Don't Hurt: The Joy of Aging Mindfully,* to him.

The line I wrote about in the week Time for Releasing from Janet Conner's book *Soul Vows* is very helpful when we are having difficulty forgiving someone.

"God loves _____ as much as God loves me."

This Week's Practice

Are you holding on to anger? Make a list of anyone toward whom you feel angry. Are you willing to let go? And if you are not willing, are you willing to pray to be willing to let go?

Spend time this week praying for the willingness to let go of your anger. Take as much time as you need to be free. Last week's metta practice works well on helping us forgive.

It feels so good to know that
God is helping me let go of all my
resentments today.

Time for Gratitude

"If the only prayer you ever say in
your entire life is thank you,
it will be enough."

—*Meister Eckhart*

G ratitude can change a mood in a split second. It can
happen so quickly it's hard to believe. We can be in
the worst of moods and it is suddenly—*poof*!—wiped out,
erased, vanished! Ralph Blum wrote that there is a calmness
to a life lived in gratitude, a quiet joy. Gratitude is like a miracle or magic or simply like an eraser.

Remember, it is our thoughts that create our feelings. If we are mindful, when we are aware that we are in a negative, angry, resentful, jealous mood, or any mood that pulls us down and makes us suffer, we can change the thought that created the feeling with gratitude. When we don't know what thought created the feeling, we simply think of something for which we are grateful.

It helps to write a daily gratitude list in the morning. And often at night, when my head is on the pillow, I breathe in and out three times and go over my day, remembering the times and the people that I am grateful for.

Remember the week on neuroplasticity? The more we practice thinking about things for which we are grateful, the deeper that groove is created in our brain so that soon gratitude will be more automatic. My friend Fran was having a very difficult time and called me. She was anxious. She couldn't stop this thinking and worrying. She projected terrible things happening to herself in the future.

I suggested she breathe in and out three times to slow down her thinking and then asked what she was grateful for. She just stopped. At first she couldn't think of a thing.

"Okay," she finally said. "I'm grateful for you."

"That's nice." I replied. "Thank you! What else?"

"Well, I have a car that runs. I have gas in my car."

"Good! Now how do you feel?"

"Much better!" she answered.

And she was. She was calm and in the moment. Something had immediately shifted when she brought her awareness to gratitude.

The other day I was in very slow traffic, almost late for an appointment. I could feel my stress growing. I said *stop* and *shhhh, Ruthie*, and felt calm. And I remembered gratitude. I looked up at the trees and thought how lucky I am to live in Florida, with trees blooming all year long. And the fact that living in Florida also brought very slow drivers became less important.

Let me close this week with this Quero Apache prayer: "Looking behind I am filled with gratitude. Looking forward I am filled with vision. Looking upwards I am filled with strength. Looking within I discover peace."

This Week's Practice

Giving thanks is scientifically proven to improve emotional and physical well-being. Opening the morning with a simple thank-you will start your day on a positive note. This week remember to make a gratitude list in the morning and before you go to sleep. As you make this more and more of a habit in your life, you'll notice that you are more grateful during the day as well. You might be filled with gratitude when you see a baby or a kitten, a beautiful scene or a flower, or when someone does something kind or helpful for you.

> *It feels so good to know that*
> *the more I practice remembering to*
> *be grateful, the better I feel.*

time to be with nature!

Time for Nature

"I thank you God for this most amazing day,
for the leaping greenly spirits of trees, and for the
blue dream of sky and for everything which is
natural, which is infinite, which is yes."

—*E. E. Cummings*

Taking time in nature can be a time for simply stopping, getting away from all the hustle and bustle, all the details and stress of everyday life. It can be a time to be with ourselves and the God of our understanding. There is nothing more relaxing than spending time in nature. It connects us spiritually to a power greater than ourselves. It quiets our minds and brings us inner peace. George Washington Carver wrote, "I love to think of nature as an unlimited broadcasting station, through which God speaks to us every hour, if we will only tune in."

Mary, a friend of mine, recently emailed to me a beautiful picture of a deer and wrote; "I go to the woods to feed my soul—and I always take my camera. Yesterday, I saw this beautiful deer just a few feet from me on the path. We stood and looked at each other with an understanding that we were sharing the woods—and the path. The moment was so special."

You never know what you might discover when you take this spiritual break. You might see a deer, as Mary did, or nothing unusual at all, simply the beauty of the ocean, the forest, the mountains, the rivers, or the desert. Wherever you go you will find yourself.

This Week's Practice

Take an hour or so this week, or longer and more often if you can, to connect with nature. You might want to reread the week on Time for Me. Simply be in nature, wherever it might be. You could go camping and stay in a tent for a week, or sit on your front lawn or in your backyard for an hour, or find a peaceful park. And if you can't be outside, look out a window and connect with the sky or any tree or flower you can see, or even a plant inside your home.

Just be, for however long. Sit, walk, climb, or swim. Look. No reading. No work. No to-do list.

You might want to journal about your experience when it is over, but not during. This time is just for you and nature.

God is helping me take some time for myself
in nature and it feels so good.

Time for Slowing Down

"People today do not know how to rest.
They fill their free time with countless diversions.
People cannot tolerate even a few minutes of
unoccupied time. They constantly need
something to look at, listen to, or talk about,
all to keep the emptiness inside from
rearing its terrifying head."

—*Thich Nhat Hanh*

Over the years that I began practicing mindfulness, I became more and more aware of how much I was rushing. I noticed my mind going from one thing to another, or repeating my to-do list over and over again. I might be in the shower and suddenly realize my brain is going ninety miles an hour. Or when I become awake in the morning I started to be aware how my first thought was my to-do list. Once I realize this, I learned to breathe in and out three times, which slows me down immediately. If I can, I grab a pen and paper and write down something I might want to remember so I won't worry I will forget it. I think my brain has created an old habit of fear that I might forget so it goes over and over the same thought to make sure the things to do remains in the forefront of my mind. This way, by writing it down, it frees me from this fear of the things I worry I won't remember and I am released from the subconscious need to think about it over and over again.

It's nice when I make the discovery that I am rushing when I am in the shower or brushing my teeth. I can then turn my attention to the water on my body or in my mouth, the smell of the soap or the toothpaste, and the sound of the water.

If I am out of doors I can look around or up and become aware of my surroundings. But no matter where I am I can use this stop and breathe technique. I bring myself to this moment . . . now . . . this breath . . . and slow down. I can become aware of my chest rising and falling, my stomach filling and emptying, and I often, without thinking, find myself smiling. What a difference!

Meditation teacher Bill Menza wrote that we are a society on the go. "We have this habit energy that tells us we have to be busy all the time. We are like rats on a treadmill."

At a recent retreat I found out how true this is! During a group sharing almost everyone talked about how they rushed—and everyone wanted to change this habit.

This Week's Practice

This is a week to be aware when you feel you are rushing. This is really a simple practice that will be helped the more you meditate and practice mindfulness. Mindfulness brings you into the present moment. You will find that the longer you develop this habit, the more quickly you will be able to slow down and experience awareness of the present moment.

As soon as you do become aware that you are rushing, use the stop and breathe practice. No matter what you are doing, stop and breathe in and out three times. This takes all of a few seconds so you *do* have time for it. This helps you stay in the present moment.

Bill Menza suggested we take a slow walk (best with nature). He wrote, "If you take a walk focus all your attention on your feet as they gently touch the ground . . . silently tell yourself as you put one foot down: *solid*. And then say it again as you place down the other one." He also suggested we sit or lie down, and focus all our attention on our breathing. Just watch your breath as you breathe in and out. Maybe linger in that space between your in-breath and your out-breath.

If you lie down you might relax your body from the top of your head all the way down to the bottom of your feet. Do this focusing 100 percent on each area and organ in your body, telling it to relax. For example, starting with your head, you can silently say: *I am aware of my head. I relax my head.* If you relax your whole body from your head to your feet, you might drift off into a very restful mind state that exists just before sleep. This mind state is supposed to be one in which many of the 37 trillion cells in your body heal and rejuvenate. Bill Menza further suggested that we notice that, when we stop and rest our body, we are also stopping a lot of our thinking, especially the negative stuff, and thus resting our mind.

I am being more and more
aware of the times I rush and am
practicing slowing down
and feeling peace.

Time for Smiling
(Even if You Don't Feel Like It)

"Sometimes your joy is the source
of your smile, but sometimes your smile
can be the source of your joy."

—*Thích Nhat Hanh*

My mother used to tell me I had such a pretty smile. "Why don't you use it more often?" she would ask, making me so self-conscious that it took me years to smile more often and naturally. There is so much positive scientific evidence about smiling that I could go on forever. But here are just a few of the many benefits: smiling lifts our mood and the moods of those around us and can even lengthen our lives. A smile can transform you and the world around you. Smiling releases neuropeptides that help us release stress. Our feel-good neurotransmitters, dopamine, endorphins, and serotonin are all released when we smile. They are also antidepressants, natural pain relievers, and help to ease anger.

Smiling relaxes our body and can lower our heart rate and blood pressure. And it's contagious! Each time you smile at a person, both your brain and the brain of the other person releases feel-good chemicals, activates reward centers, makes you both more attractive, and increases the chances of you living longer, healthier lives. The person receiving the smile (subconsciously) will want to smile in return, thus creating the same chemical effects on both of your bodies.

Babies start smiling as newborns and even blind babies smile, so it is not something we learn but it is a natural behavior. It is said that your body doesn't know the difference between something real or something imagined. Smiling can "trick" your body into helping you change your mood. Smiles are the most easily recognizable facial expression. People can recognize smiles from up to many feet away.

I love what my friend Nicki told me. She often practices smiling at people as part of her daily service. She said that many recent conversations about race have revealed that racism is sometimes experienced through subtle daily slights, such as an older white lady frowning at a young black man and holding her pocketbook tighter. Instead, she likes to smile at people, especially those who look different from her, and catch their eyes. It's a way of saying, "Welcome, I'm glad you're on the bike path/in the grocery line/at the stoplight today. We have a friendly neighborhood."

Mindfulness practice brings us closer to our feelings in the present moment. As we learn to accept (rather than resist) who we are, we begin to soften and let go of our suffering. So in this respect, smiling will be more of a natural part of our lives.

Recently I suggested to a friend who was feeling depressed that she end her night and begin her morning with a smile and say to herself, *Something good is going to happen to me today.* She emailed me a few evenings later: "Going to bed to wait for tomorrow's smile and next good thing. That feels so good to say." I emailed back, "This is lovely. What you wrote triggered my smile! Much gratitude!"

This Week's Practice

Creating a new habit of smiling more often is not easy for those of us who haven't been used to it. Remember it is said that 50 percent of our personalities are genetic, some are added as we grow up, and 30 to 40 percent can be developed.

Smiling when it didn't feel natural to me felt very awkward and unnatural at first. But as I began to change and become a happier person, I'm happy to say more smiles just showed up.

So practice this week even if it feels awkward or uncomfortable. We can develop the habit of smiling before we fall asleep at night, and making an intention to smile as we greet each morning before we do anything else.

We can decide to smile at our neighbors, store clerks, and other people we see on a regular basis. We can smile at strangers!

When your head is on the pillow each night, smile. Expect something good to happen to you tomorrow. If you should wake up during the night, smile. Expect something good to happen to you the next day. When you wake up in the morning, smile. Expect something good to happen to you today.

The more we practice, our brains will change and we will find ourselves smiling spontaneously more often. Even if you don't feel like it, fake it until you make it! It will change how you feel.

God is helping me to remember
to smile more often and that helps me
to feel happier and full of joy.

Time for Happiness

"Happiness is like a butterfly which,
when pursued, is always beyond our grasp,
but, if you will sit down quietly,
may alight upon you."

—*Nathaniel Hawthorne*

The new science of neuroplasticity teaches us that we can be happy even if we were not born with this tendency. I wasn't! Many years ago, and before I was a daily meditator, it used to take me three cups of coffee to even talk in the morning while my ex-husband would be cheerful and smiling and ready to start his day. My son Bob was the same way—an instant smile on his face, even as a baby.

Author Rick Hanson tells us that positive emotions strengthen our immune system, reduce stress, foster healthier and longer lives, and even protect our heart. He defines positive and good as what leads to happiness for ourself and others, while negative and bad mean leading to suffering and harm.

As we have been learning through the previous weeks in this book, there are so many ways we can create happiness in our lives. The most obvious is doing the things we love, being in places that we love, being with people whom we love, and helping others. While we can be happy with all this, we are depending on outside things to make us happy and our practice is learning to change so that happiness comes from the inside. So as we learn to give up habits that make us suffer, we can practice "stop" when we are angry or hear our negative thoughts, and practice faith instead of fear. Our daily meditation practice and being mindful throughout the day are some more of the ways we are learning to be happy. We are deepening our brain's path to happiness. What a gift this is!

I think we quoted this in the compassion week, but it's worth seeing again. The Dalai Lama said, "If you want others to be happy, practice compassion. If you want to be happy, practice compassion."

This Week's Practice

Each one of the past weeks' practice has been teaching us how to become happy, peaceful, and free from suffering. Keep doing just what you have been doing! Even when you have practiced all the "time fors" in this book. You can always go back to any week to reinforce your happiness. This is a lifetime practice that gets easier and easier as you create these new habits, these new pathways in your brain.

As we make mindfulness a lifetime practice, we become more aware of any negativity we still have about ourselves and others. Remember to be consistent with morning prayer and meditation, and saying *stop* or *shhhh* when you get into your negative stories in your head. It is the second thought that counts. Quickly switch from the negative thought to a positive affirmation. Don't forget your daily gratitude list and self-compassion.

These are musts for happiness. They eventually become habits and take no effort at all. We can add a number of other practices to this list as they feel appropriate.

I am practicing all the things
I am learning to be a happier person
and this feels wonderful!

Time for Connection

"The things that matter most
in our lives are not fantastic or grand.
They are the moments when we
touch one another."

—*Jack Kornfield*

There is something very special that happens when we feel connected to another person. It can transpire when we simply smile at a stranger, when our eyes meet, and she returns the smile. It can happen when we are having a deep conversation with a friend, when both of our attentions are solely on each other, not diluted by a disturbance or an off-the-subject thought.

When we feel connected we might smile without thinking. We might feel warm around our heart center. Our thoughts slow down. We might not even have any thoughts and we are simply one with the other person in the moment. We feel connected when we visit a sick friend or bring flowers to someone we love. It happens when we give someone a compliment or encourage someone who is afraid or needs their spirit lifted. It happens when we share a special moment with someone who means a lot to us, such as watching a sunset together or going for a walk in the park.

We feel connected when we join with like-minded people such as a club, a self-help group, a temple, mosque or church, sangha, a sorority or fraternity. We don't even have to be with another person to feel connected. We can feel it when we write a letter or send a text or email to someone we care about, or spend time in a store looking for the perfect gift for a sick friend. All we have to do is take our time and see the person in our mind.

Hugs are wonderful ways to feel connected. There's a saying that we can't give a hug without getting one back. Even a handshake connects us to the other person and in time can lead to a hug.

And we feel connected when we are on the receiving end of the smile, the hug, the gift, the compliment, the encouragement, the letter, email, or text. Our lives are made richer and more meaningful by our connections. Many of these moments are special and often remembered for a long time or even throughout our lives.

This Week's Practice

This can be an especially heart-warming week. Take time to connect and feel the connection.

Do at least one of these each day:

Send a birthday, get well, or congratulations card.

Send a letter, email, or text to someone you haven't connected with in a while.

Go to lunch or dinner with someone you care about.

Do something special with someone you care about.

Dig out some old pictures and put them in an album or on your computer. Relive the memories.

Pick up the phone and connect with a family member or dear friend.

You can add more to this list as you go along. Just remember, one activity each day—at least!

My heart feels so full when I connect with someone I like. I am making a commitment to do it more often.

Time for Change

"And suddenly you know:
It's time to start something new and
trust the magic of beginnings."

—*Meister Eckhart*

This week is a good time for us to consider what might not be working in our lives. We might be trying to make something work that has long outgrown its usefulness and it keeps us stuck from moving forward. I know I have a few of these . . . still trying to make something work that stopped working a while ago.

Maybe you've heard the saying, "God never closes one door without opening another." Trust that you are not alone; God is working in your life.

Read the questions on the practice page carefully and give them some serious thought. If things feel as if they are falling apart, maybe it is just time for a new beginning. A wise person wrote:

> If your life starts to dismantle,
> just breathe and let it happen.
> There is a season for all things.
> When a season comes to an end,
> it means that it has fulfilled its purpose.
> And now it's time for change!
> Don't hold on to yesterday!
> Let the winds carry you into tomorrow.
>
> —Author Unknown

Let go, have faith, and let it happen!

This Week's Practice

Spend some time this first day examining the questions on the following page. Read them slowly. Meditate on them. Journal about them. Talk them over with a trusted friend.

Is there something you're holding on to?

Have you tried too long to make something work?

Are you afraid you'll miss something if you let go?

Has what you are holding on to outlived its usefulness?

Are you afraid to try something new?

Are you afraid of change?

Are you afraid that if you let go you'll lose something important?

Read these questions again each morning this week and, as you go about your days, be mindful of any feeling of fear that might arise from whatever it is you are holding on to. And while letting go might contain some fear, soon you can discover that the fear changes to excitement. Don't plan a lot of details just yet. Let the future unfold as you begin to learn that by releasing what you are holding on to, new doors open and make way for new possibilities, new beginnings.

All the energies of the universe are
giving me the courage to
let go and change.

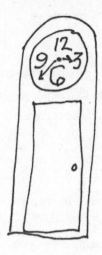

Time for Now

"The moment your attention turns to the *now*,
you feel a presence, a stillness, a peace . . .
as soon as you honor the present moment, all
unhappiness and struggle dissolve, and life
begins to flow with joy and ease. Stress is caused
by being here but wanting to be there.
Not accepting what is now. Judging it.
Wanting it to be different."

—*Eckhart Tolle*

Please read the first two lines of the quote on the previous page *slowly*. Doesn't that make you feel peaceful? Just stay with that feeling for a moment. While it is unrealistic, in fact impossible to feel like this all the time, wouldn't it be wonderful if you could feel like this more and more often? If you have been diligently practicing the previous weeks, you most likely do have more peace in your life. Now you know how much your thoughts create your feelings and how you can be in charge of your thoughts. Now you know you can choose your thoughts. As Thich Nhat Hanh teaches us, "Whether this moment is happy or not depends on you. It's you who makes the moment happy. It's not the moment that makes you happy. With mindfulness, concentration, and insight, any moment can become a happy moment. Happiness is an art."

We have to practice bringing our awareness to each moment. We learn to identify the thought that creates the feeling and in that moment, if it creates suffering, we can let it go. We can be in the peace and joy of the moment. For example, let's say you are looking at a sunset. It's possible to just be with the experience without a thought. But very likely you will be aware of yourself saying something like, "How beautiful!" Being aware, you can see that you just had a thought about the sunset. When you let go of the thought, you can once again enjoy the sunset. As we learn to detach from the thought we become the observer of the thought and we feel peace. Abraham Maslow writes, "I can feel guilty about the past, apprehensive about the future, but only in the present can I act. The ability to be in the present moment is a major component of mental wellness."

Let's imagine that suddenly there is a sound, a buzzing sound, and you look around. Within an instant a bee is circling around you and the rose you were enjoying. "Damn!" you yell, and your mind breaks the special moment. Your feelings change instantly and you are filled with fear and disappointment. Instead of letting your thoughts go into long stories, you can bring your awareness back to what you were doing. Rather than letting those new feelings take over, you can come right back into the now, the present moment, by stopping, bringing your awareness back to your breath and smiling. Staying calm, the bee will be less likely to bother you, and you would be getting a wonderful lesson in the art of happiness. You'll find that when you bring your awareness to your breath, you are just here, in the now, in the present moment, and you feel peace.

My friend Lee Purser tells us, "The moment we turn our attention to this moment right now, we enter the mystery of the unknown. We become explorers, with fresh eyes, ears, smells, tastes, touch, body, open minds, never knowing what we will find. We can start with our breath, noticing it magically entering our nose, lungs, chest, bellies, with no effort on our part, and then just as magically leaving the same way. We can notice, sense, rest in the pause at the end of the inhale, nothing going on, then the magic when all of a sudden the new breath rushes in. If one can let go of the needing-to-know mind we can relax deeply into life unfolding right before our eyes, ears, nose, tongue, touch, body, mind."

This Week's Practice

Practice being aware of exactly what you are doing during the following activities:

Washing the dishes, taking a shower, brushing your teeth.

Hearing the water. Smelling the soap, the toothpaste. Tasting the toothpaste.

Walking. Feeling your feet on the ground, your arms moving.

Driving. Feeling your hands on the steering wheel, your body in the seat.

Breathing in. Breathing out. Being with this breath and not knowing what the next breath will bring you.

Whatever you are doing, simply be there.

Fully.

Focusing only on what you are doing.

Only.

Ahhh . . . peace.

> *It is so peaceful to be aware of*
> *this breath, expecting nothing, knowing*
> *nothing but what I discover in this moment.*
> *It feels so good to know that I have*
> *everything I need in the moment.*

Time for Acceptance

> "And acceptance is the answer to all my
> problems today. When I am disturbed it is because
> I find some person, place, thing or situation—
> some fact of my life—unacceptable to me, and I
> can find no serenity until I can accept that person,
> place, thing or situation as being exactly the
> way it is supposed to be at this moment."
>
> —*The Big Book of Alcoholics Anonymous*

One day a friend sent me a quote via email by Pema Chö-drön: "Nothing ever really goes away until it teaches us what we really need to know." This resounded within me as it was so true. There was something I had not been able to let go of, no matter how hard I tried. I wanted something to be different than it was, and no matter what I did to let it go, it still troubled me.

A few minutes later MJ, another friend, sent me an email, which turned out to be the solution I needed to hear. She worked as a hospice counselor, and part of her job was to visit patients in nursing homes. She soon observed that some patients were very calm and agreeable no matter what was going on around them or happening to them. She felt a different energy when she entered their rooms. And it was clear that the staff enjoyed visiting these patients even if some were bedridden and spoke very little. She began to ask these patients how they were able to maintain such contentment in their surroundings. Each answer was different but the theme was the same: deep acceptance of what is. One day she had the privilege of visiting people who were totally free of any concern. The experience of this gift transformed her own practice ever since—and helped me.

Deepak Chopra wrote that acceptance means that we make the following commitment: "Today I will accept people, situations, circumstances, and events as they occur." He went on to say, "this means this moment is as it should be, because the whole universe is as it should be." After reading this one morning, I made the decision to be more mindful about how I accepted things. That very morning I found out that I had missed an important call a few days earlier, a message that my proof was ready at the printers and I needed to okay a proof for the imprinting of a CD. By being so late, I wouldn't get the imprinted CDs in time for a retreat I was leading the following week. My first reaction was anger. They should have called me back when I didn't return the call! Why didn't they just fax it to me! They could have emailed it to me! All this time I was very aware that I was not accepting the situation and, while being angry, I actually smiled. I let myself feel the feelings until they softened and disappeared and was able to see the lesson in it.

In her research, author Brené Brown found that at the heart of compassionate people was acceptance: "The better we are at accepting ourselves and others, the more compassionate we become." *Ahhh* . . . acceptance of what is. Not what I want them to be. Just what I needed. Just what we all need!

This Week's Practice

Is there something you're holding on to, something you can't let go of? Be mindful of how you feel when it comes up for you. Do you feel peaceful or does it cause you suffering? Stay with the feelings each time they appear. Ask yourself,

Is this how I want to feel? If the answer is no, then pray for the willingness to let go. And remember your God box or God can!

The Serenity Prayer

God, grant me the serenity
to accept the things
I cannot change,
Courage to change the
things I can, and the
wisdom to know the difference.

—Reinhold Niebuhr

*It feels so good to know
that God is helping me accept the
things I cannot change.*

Time for Shame

"Anyone who has never made a mistake
has never tried anything new."

—*Albert Einstein*

Your first thought might be, *Why would I want shame for a week? That's certainly not something that is going to give me joy or peace. Ahhh* . . . but you are so wrong. We need to look at our shame, any shame we still have that is buried within us, shine a light of mindfulness, honesty, and acceptance on it; bring it to the surface and let it go. That's where the peace and joy come in, when we are free from our shame.

We can feel shame for two reasons. One is for something we have done to ourselves or someone else. If this is the case, we'll free ourselves by making amends.

The second type of shame is sometimes a bit more difficult to recognize. It is shame that comes from a feeling created by the thoughts we have interpreted or judged. For example, we might think people don't like us or perceive we are not as good as someone else. We might feel shame that we gave the wrong answer in school and we think the others think we are stupid. Perhaps we weren't chosen for a job or to be on a team or we failed at something. There are so many more reasons we can feel shame. We might have false perceptions about something that happened in the past.

The steps below in this week's practice will bring great joy and peace as you experience freedom from shame.

This Week's Practice

Begin with small steps this week. Spend some time in meditation to allow yourself to look at some of the shame you might be carrying. Write down those troubling thoughts that come up right away. Once you deal with these, one at a time, you can go deeper.

We can use the tools of sharing, journaling, accepting, and praying. Sharing with a trusted friend, sponsor, mentor, or spiritual advisor to express and empty is so important. If you are not ready to share this we can do the same by expressing and emptying in our journals. There is tremendous freedom in hearing or seeing our truth. We need to look directly at it with acceptance, not judgment. If we see we need to take an action step such as making amends, we should do this as quickly as possible.

And finally, we can pray to have our shame removed.

This is one of those "time fors" that might not be completed in a week. It's most likely going to take longer. That's perfectly fine. You can come back to it anytime. Other week's exercises might trigger a memory of a new shame. More will be revealed in the process of life itself. Take care of them as they come up. If you find this too much to handle alone, please get help from a therapist.

It would be helpful to go back and reread the week of metta loving-kindness. Here is a variation of it:

May I be happy.

May I be peaceful.

May I forgive myself and others.

May I be free from all shame.

May I be free from suffering.

It is so freeing to know that my
Higher Power is helping me do what
I have to do to release
all my shame.

Time for Impermanence

"To everything there is a season . . ."

—*Ecclesiastes*

One of the most important Buddhist teachings is that of *impermanence*. Everything eventually changes. Nothing is permanent. We suffer because we try to hold on to everything that makes us happy or that we think makes us happy. We struggle to hold on to all the pleasant aspects of our lives. We resist change—yet there is nothing we can do about it. Thus, we suffer. We suffer when we lose a job or a loved one, when a friend moves away, or when our children leave home.

We suffer when we think life isn't fair, or that a situation shouldn't have happened, that the good things should last forever. We might even suffer when a favorite TV program goes off the air or when our most comfortable sweater is no longer wearable. Our suffering ends when we can accept impermanence. Then can we experience inner peace.

There are good, more acceptable, even joyful aspects of impermanence. A broken arm heals. Wars end. Our losing team wins the pennant the following year. Seeds become flowers and our babies graduate from college, get married, and have babies.

We can even be grateful for impermanence! What if an acorn stayed an acorn and didn't grow into a beautiful oak tree? What if our child went to kindergarten and never grew beyond that? What if morning didn't change into evening didn't change into night didn't change into morning? Just to name a few!

On the other hand we grow older and lose body strength. Aches and pains are with us more frequently. Our hair turns white or gray and even our smooth skin changes! And we experience the impermanence of our memory. Where did I put the car keys? What was his name? How did I forget that dentist appointment?

Kathleen Dowling Singh asks us, "If we remembered that our breaths were numbered, what would our relationship be to this breath right now?" When I read this for the first time I stopped and thought about this deeply. It was Patriot's Day, one year after the tragedy at the Boston Marathon. A powerful example of impermanence. Happy, excited people suddenly experiencing tragedy, death, lost limbs. The phrase Boston Strong had been coined to represent how the people in Boston came together to support each other through this tragedy. I was taking the morning off because of the deep feelings I had about this day. Although I now lived in Florida, my heart was still in Boston. I had lived in Massachusetts all but fifteen years of my life.

I stayed with this awareness the rest of the day. I was aware of how I spoke to people, aware of catching myself rushing so I slowed myself down, aware of being a good listener to the woman I was meeting later that afternoon. This could be my last day. How did I want to spend it?

Let's think about this. Stop. Right now. This breath is numbered. If we have only a certain amount of time to live, how do we want to spend it?

This is not to say that we won't suffer when a loved one dies, or be upset if the company we work for lets us go, or experience the multitude of other painful things that happen in the natural course of life. We must go through our grief or our upset or our disappointment in order to move on, as our grief or upset or disappointment is also impermanent.

The Dalai Lama tells us that awareness of impermanence is encouraged, so that when it is coupled with our appreciation of the enormous potential of our human existence, it will give us a sense of urgency that we must use every precious moment.

This Week's Practice

Take some time to watch your breath and your feelings. As we deepen our mindfulness practice, we can begin to see how everything changes moment to moment. Even our breath changes—first a long breath, then a short breath, a deep breath, and then a shallow breath. Feelings might be up one moment and down the next and then neutral. Anger changes into forgiveness into peace. Please stop and take some time to examine your feelings about impermanence.

What do you like about impermanence?

What do you fear about impermanence?

Examine what changes you might be resisting in your life.

Make a list of changes that are happening in your life that you don't like or want.

Then make a list of the things in your life that you want to stay forever. Is there anything you can do about them?

If there isn't, can you accept them and then let go?

If you can't let go, can you notice your resistance and your suffering about this?

Ask yourself if this is how you want to feel. Is your struggle to accept change worth the suffering?

Some time ago I was going through a difficult time and my teacher Joanne Friday suggested I read The Five Remembrances of Buddhism each morning. At first I found them very depressing and I dreaded reading them. But soon I began to see them as just a part of life, and my fear of loss began to leave me.

The Five Remembrances

1. I am of the nature to grow old. There is no way to escape growing old.

2. I am of the nature to have ill health. There is no way to escape having ill health.

3. I am of the nature to die. There is no way to escape death.

4. All that is dear to me and everyone I love are of the nature to change. There is no way to escape being separate from them.

5. My actions are my only true belongings. I cannot escape the consequences of my actions. My actions are the ground upon which I stand.

It would be a good practice to read this for a while every morning and notice how, over time, your appreciation of life changes and your suffering lessens and lessens.

My life is flowing like a river
as I watch every happening in the
natural order of things, and
this feels so right.

Time for Rethinking

"Before the thought, you weren't suffering;
with the thought, you're suffering;
when you recognize the thought isn't true,
again there is no suffering."

—*Byron Katie*

There was a time when I was asked often to speak at a meditation group to which I belonged. Preparing for these talks required a great deal of time but I did enjoy doing the speaking and it made me feel a part of the group to be asked. Suddenly I was no longer invited to speak. New people had joined the group and now they were the ones being asked. This really bothered me.

Old feelings from childhood were being triggered. Wasn't I good enough? Were they better than me? What was wrong with me? I wasn't able to get any answers.

While this was going on, I was also busy writing a new book and facilitating retreats and workshops. Then I was relieved of another job I had been doing for the group for over four years, so that a new person could have the opportunity to serve. This felt more like a relief and I smiled. It gave me extra time to work on the book! I soon saw how I had been attached to the speaking and was able to see that not being asked was also a gift. When I turned this around, the heaviness of rejection left me. I smiled and felt a great sense of joy.

I heard author and speaker, Sonia Ricotti, once say there are just two things: you and something happening outside of you. It is your thought about what's happening outside of you that makes you feel the way you feel. She said that is the equivalent to staring at a closed door that is locked and you are not going anywhere. She suggested asking, "What's the silver lining here? What are the opportunities here? What are the open doors around you?"

Life changes. Nothing stays the same. Friends leave. Children grow up and move. New opportunities come into our lives. Other people are even chosen over us! When we can simply accept what is, without all the thoughts that are triggered by these changes, we can feel peace and joy. Holding on to how things were creates suffering. Accepting the inevitable changes, discovering new doors where old ones were closed, finding the silver linings, can be a challenge, but the practice is well worth it. All of these are more examples of last week's study on impermanence.

This Week's Practice

Take some time to see if you are holding on to any regrets. Watch your thinking carefully. What are your thoughts when you are disappointed in something, when things don't go the way you want them to go? What happens when the stock market is up or down, when someone might leave you out, when the bills come in, or you don't receive the phone call you've been waiting for?

Be aware that it is only your thoughts that make you suffer and look for the silver lining. Author Alan Cohen wrote, "Imagine that life is working in your favor even when it appears to be working against you." Remember that it's the second thought that counts!

*I no longer listen to the first thought when it
makes me suffer. I remember it's the second thought
that counts and this makes me smile.*

Time for Mistakes

"Some of the most comforting words
in the universe are 'me, too.' That moment
when you find out that your struggle is
also someone else's struggle, that you are
not alone, and that others have
been down the same road."

—*Unknown Sage*

I once went to a workshop on finances and was so relieved
to find that everyone had money concerns, from the
lawyer, the accountant, the teacher, and someone who was

unemployed. It was not just me! I had gone into the workshop feeling a bit embarrassed to admit how concerned I could be and not sure how much I would share. I left the workshop much lighter in the knowledge that my concerns were shared by so many others.

I love the quote that opens this week because it shows us that when we share what bothers us with others, not only are we helping ourselves, but we help others, too. It shows how we all struggle with one thing or another and we are not alone.

It reminds me of another quote I saw recently by John C. Maxwell, "God uses people who fail because there aren't any other kind." So please don't worry about your imperfections or failing or making a mistake! We all make them! And if you don't try, you'll never grow. And if you do fail, you can always share the experience with others, helping to give them the confidence to try something new.

It's the holding on to the mistakes and beating ourselves up over and over again that causes our suffering—and it's when our mistakes make us afraid to try something again. When we stay stuck because we are afraid of failing, we hold ourselves back from living up to our full potential. We deserve better than this!

✳ This Week's Practice

It's said we learn from our mistakes. Take some time to think about the mistakes you made in your life and see if you can find lessons in them. How have past mistakes affected your life? Have they held you back from taking chances?

Be aware this week of any new mistakes you make and look for lessons in them. Be mindful of any time you think about doing or saying something, and then hold back for fear of the results. What's holding you back? What are you afraid of? Is it the fear of what someone will say, or how it will be judged?

Remind yourself that if you don't try new things, nothing will change. What does failure mean to you? Take a chance this week on doing, creating, or trying something new, perhaps something you have wanted to do for a long time but held back from doing for whatever reason. Go beyond fear. Do it anyway! Remember, you're not alone in your feelings.

Praying for courage can really help. And when you feel up to it, and you know another person is struggling with some mistake you have made, share your story with them. Not only will you be helping them but you will feel good about yourself!

It's exciting to move beyond the fear
of failure and making mistakes, self-doubts,
and worries about what other people might think,
and take chances in my life today.
I pray for the courage to live my life to
the fullest and be all I can be.

Time for Choosing

"Managing the power of choice,
with all its creative and spiritual implications,
is the essence of human experience."

—*Carolyn Myss*

It's time to know we really have a choice as to how we feel. With all the new scientific information being discovered on neuroplasticity, we can no longer think that we cannot change our patterns of thinking. The adage "You can't teach an old dog new tricks" does not apply.

At a retreat I attended, our teacher, Fred Eppsteiner, used a wonderful example of what to imagine so we can screen our thoughts. He had us picture the gatekeeper of a community. He often had a list of acceptable people and when a car pulled up at the gate, he would check his list and say whether someone could come in or not.

This can be the same with our thoughts. There is no stopping a thought from coming up to the gate. Because of habit energy, our history, our perceptions, and beliefs, thoughts will come in, but we have a choice as to whether they stay or not.

I was once very upset over an argument I had with someone. For two days my mind went over and over the words that were used. I was holding on to my anger and judgments by going over and over again the same story of what was said. On the third morning, I was aware of how tense I was. I was still angry and right before I meditated, I asked myself, *Is this how I want to feel?* The answer was loud and clear. *No!* I began to say a loving-kindness prayer for that person and myself:

May I be happy.
May I be peaceful.
May I be free from suffering.

And then:

May you be happy.
May you be peaceful.
May you be free of suffering.

Within seconds I was smiling and at peace. I had let go. I was free from my story. It was over.

"Is this how I want to feel?" is a very powerful question. "Who do I want to let in my life?" is another good question. Who are your friends? Are they supportive? Are they kind? Do they share the same values? Should the gatekeeper let them in your life?

One of the obstacles to change is, of course, fear. It is said that people often stay with the difficult life because it is something they know, rather than making a change for something they don't know.

Change requires courage and oftentimes faith. Faith is the other side of fear. An acronym for fear is False Evidence Appearing Real. Another good saying is "Faith is fear that has said its prayers."

Like last week, when you read not to let your mistakes hold you back, this week concentrate on and practice not letting your fear hold you back.

This Week's Practice

It's good to know that we almost always have a choice. We can change our job, our career, our friends, our partners, and even our sex. We can change our thoughts and, as we have learned, we can even change the pathways in our brain.

You have been practicing for some time now watching your thoughts and changing them from negative to positive, from the thoughts that bring you suffering to thoughts that bring you joy. So certainly continue with this.

Also spend time this week looking at the parts of your life that are not the way you would like them to be. Is it time for change? What can you change to improve it? Does fear hold you back?

Change takes time. Let this be a thoughtful week, one when you are observing, thinking, considering. You don't necessarily have to take actions steps to make any significant changes. Only when you are ready. You can use the God bag. You can pray for guidance. You can get help from someone you trust.

It feels so good to know
I can choose how I want to feel today.
I can choose peace, love, joy,
and happiness.

Time for Grieving

"Only intimacy with the Self will
bring about true healing."

—*Deepak Chopra*

There are many reasons to grieve: the loss of a job, a broken toy, failing health, declining energy as we age, the death of a close friend, an unfulfilled dream, the passing of a beloved pet, the heart-breaking loss of someone we love dearly. Each one touches us in its own unique way. Some losses take over our lives for a long time; others hurt for a moment or a day or two and then we move on.

How we deal with each loss is very personal. Elisabeth Kübler-Ross helped us to understand grief when she came out with her famous five stages of grief back in the 1960's. She was a Swiss-American psychiatrist, a pioneer in near-death studies, and the author of the groundbreaking book, *On Death and Dying*, where she first discussed her theories. They are universal and are experienced by people from all walks of life.

The five stages do not necessarily occur in any specific order. We often move between stages before achieving a more peaceful acceptance of death. Some of us don't have the luxury of time required to achieve the final stage of grief. Some of us tough it through, pushing down our feelings and going on as if nothing happened, leaving the feelings stuck, only to show up at unexpected times. Some people will wear their emotions on their sleeves and be outwardly emotional. Others will experience their grief more internally, and may not cry. Please don't judge how you or anyone else experiences grief, as each person will experience it differently.

The stages are:

1. Denial and isolation
2. Anger
3. Bargaining
4. Depression
5. Acceptance

I cried very rarely a few weeks after I lost my son. I was numb. I attended Compassionate Friends, a wonderful support group for those who have lost children or siblings. I went to my twelve-step group every day, and saw a therapist twice a week for a while. I poured my heart out in my computer, journaling about my feelings for over a year and a half. My partner was completely there for me. When she held me, I cried. And I had a good friend, Andy, who had lunch with me once a week. She would ask, "How are you, *really*?" and just let me talk. A few years later I attended a workshop facilitated by Steven Levine and his wife Ondrea. It was for therapists and I thought I was going for the purpose of helping other people. Around 400 people attended. Steven asked how many people had lost a child and I was amazed when around forty people raised their hands!

A microphone was set up and those of us who had questions lined up. My question was about my concern that I rarely cried and I thought something was wrong with me. Ondrea's response really helped me. She asked if I cried often when other sad things happened to me and I said I didn't. Truth is, I cry at commercials and other moving or heartwarming times, but not often about my own life. She asked what I did to cope and when I told her she assured me that we all grieve differently, and that I had used other methods to heal. So please remember that coping with loss is very personal.

This Week's Practice
(and for as Long as You Need It)

It's suggested that the best thing you can do is to allow yourself to feel the grief as it comes over you. Resisting it only will prolong the natural process of healing.

Depending on the extent of your loss, the following can be very helpful: journaling, talking, therapy, support groups (for a death of a child or a sibling I highly recommend Compassionate Friends), religious or spiritual readings. Time in nature can also be very soothing and comforting.

Take as much time as you need to take. Don't push down or ignore your feelings but express them in any way that you can.

I am taking all the time I need to heal.
It feels so good to know God is there
for me and comforting me.

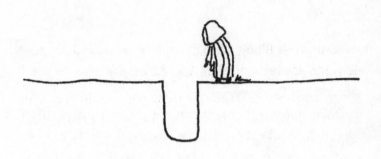

Time for Nothing

"You may be great at doing everything, but if you cannot do nothing, you have not achieved mastery."

—*Alan Cohen*

"Why would I want to do nothing?" you might ask. "So far, each week this book asks me to do something, take an action step, make a change, or gives me something to think about. And now *nothing*? Seems too easy!"

And yet, doing nothing is not easy for many of us. We usually have a long to-do list with much to accomplish. Or you might find doing nothing is boring. We're so used to doing *something*. We fill up our days with busyness and when we don't have something specific to do we watch TV or check our email or Facebook.

Doing nothing is not the same as the week we practiced silence. We can be active when we are silent. We can be washing the dishes or making a bed. We can be meditating or we can be polishing our car or weeding our garden. We can even be working! Or, yes, we can be doing nothing in silence. But doing nothing is passive. There's nothing to accomplish, nothing to do but just be.

I'm not suggesting that you do nothing for an entire week. That would be almost impossible and unreasonable, unless you went away to a retreat or a cave, or decided to have a retreat at home. But choose to take some time each day, depending on the commitments you have for the day. You could take fifteen minutes. You could take an hour. And each day can be a different length of time, depending on what is going on in your life that particular day. For example, you could take a slow walk around the block or sit at the beach just looking at the water. There are many more suggestions on the This Week's Practice page.

Stopping and doing nothing is helpful if you find yourself anxious, uptight, or overwhelmed. It gives your mind a chance to settle down and come to a place of peace, as well as a time to rest your body. If you should find yourself anxious because you do have a lot to do and doing nothing creates more stress, simply do nothing for a short time. Notice your reactions. Make friends with them. You can say something to your anxious self something like *It's okay. We're just resting for a few minutes. This is healthy!*

It's a wonderful opportunity to practice being mindful, to simply be in the moment, to be fully aware of how you feel and what is going on around you. It's a wonderful chance to be in touch with yourself.

This Week's Practice

You could look out your window and watch the sunrise or sunset if you can't get outside. Inside or outside you can look at the moon and stars or watch the clouds drift by or watch the snow or rain fall.

You could sit in a rocking chair and just rock. You could lounge in the bathtub or hot tub. You could swing or sit in a glider. I am sure you can find many more ways to do nothing, just relax, just be.

You might want to journal each day when you finish your "doing nothing time." Was it boring? Was it peaceful? Did it get better as the days passed? Did you discover new things about yourself? Did it change the way you felt the rest of the day? Did you resist doing it? Did you look forward to this time?

Remember, there are no right or wrongs, no judging good or bad. Simply describe your experience. It might become a lifetime practice!

> *It feels so good to stop, rest, and do nothing.*
> *I can feel my mind and body slowing down.*
> *I am at peace.*

time to eat!

Time for Eating

"This food is a gift from the whole universe,
the Earth, the sky, and much labor and suffering.
May we be worthy to receive it. May we take
only those foods which promote health and
well-being. May we eat only enough food and be
aware of our greed. May the benefit from
this food be used to help all sentient beings
find peace and happiness."

—*Thich Nhat Hanh*

Eating mindfully is a wonderful way to help develop the habit of being in the present moment. It helps us to slow down. We can be aware of how our food tastes instead of just rushing through our meal. It can be an enriching experience whether we're alone or with someone else.

Mindful eating also helps us to be reflective and be aware of how connected we are with everyone. There are so many people that participated in the process of the food on your table. Imagine all the people it took to bring you your food. There are those who prepare the soil, plant the seeds, harvest the plants, transport the food to be processed and packed. Then those who transport it to the store and the people who unpack the boxes and put the food on shelves or in refrigerated cases. We could go on and on to include the people who make the trucks used for shipping, the material for the trucks, the people who discovered the technology for the safety of our food, even those involved with making the tables and chairs, silverware, and napkins!

Imagine how interconnected we all are! If it weren't for other people we would either starve or have to plant and harvest and prepare everything we eat. If we are eating with another person or other people, the awareness can bring a strong sense of closeness between us. Bringing mindfulness into our meals helps to increase our sense of gratitude as well.

Here is a wonderful prayer written by meditation teacher and author Thich Nhat Hanh. It's nice to recite this alone or with others before eating.

The Five Contemplations

This food is the gift of the whole universe: the Earth, the sky, numerous living beings, and much hard, loving work.

May we eat in mindfulness and gratitude so as to be worthy to receive it.

May we recognize and transform our unwholesome mental formations, especially our greed, and learn to eat with moderation.

May we keep our compassion alive by eating in such a way that we reduce the suffering of living beings, preserve our planet, and reverse the process of global warming. We accept this food so that we may nurture our sisterhood and brotherhood, strengthen our community, and nourish our ideal of serving all living beings.

—From The Mindfulness Bell website,
by Thich Nhat Hanh

This Week's Practice

You might want to begin by practicing mindful eating one meal a week and see what a difference it makes in your life! Begin by turning off the television and all other electronic devices. Please don't read or answer the phone. It's time to be with yourself, or the other people who are sharing this meal with you.

Start with reciting the Five Contemplations from the previous page, either aloud or to yourself, or say any other prayer that might speak to you. Then think of all the people who have been involved with bringing your food to your table with gratitude.

At retreats we eat very slowly, bringing our awareness to one bite at a time. We put a forkful in our mouths, put the fork down, and put our hands in our laps, not picking up our fork again until we have chewed and swallowed what is in our mouths. This might not be practical for you if you don't have a lot of time, but if you do, it's very peaceful and refreshing.

This is a practice you might want to make a part of your life from now on.

It feels so good to eat mindfully at least
one meal this week, and to remember
and thank all those who made
my meal possible.

yes
i
did.

Time for Honesty

"Your problem is how you are
going to spend this one and precious life
you have been issued. Whether you're going to
spend it trying to look good and creating
the illusion that you have power over
circumstances, or whether you are going
to taste it, enjoy it and find out the
truth about who you are."

—*Anne Lamott*

Being honest and not stealing is certainly one part of honesty. To hide who we are and represent ourselves as otherwise is another.

Acting "as if," for instance, when we walk around looking self-assured and confident when, in actuality, we are fearful or angry, is not really being dishonest, and can lead to feeling better about ourselves. But this becomes dishonest when we hide our fears from our partner or best friend or most important, from ourselves. To be honest is to be able to say, "This is who I am," no matter how frightening it is to admit this.

What are we afraid of or ashamed to admit? That we were abused, drink or drug too much, had an abortion, are really gay, spent time in jail, or simply feel not good enough or less than? Being honest goes hand in hand with being courageous. Often we must develop our courage muscles to be able to tell the truth about who we are, first to ourselves and then to just one other human being. Jean Shinoda Bolen says that "When you find the courage to speak the truth, you begin to liberate yourself from the past that otherwise holds you hostage."

I saw a calligraphy by Thich Nhat Hanh recently, which read:

Be Beautiful
Be Yourself

This really struck a chord with me. Many years ago, when I was early in recovery, I heard a man say that he hoped he would really be himself by the time he was ten years sober. And I remember thinking something like, *I'm not going to wait that long. I want to be able to stand naked on a rooftop and shout THIS IS ME! by the time I am three years sober.*

And now, many, many years later I found myself questioning myself. Am I truly honest? Have I grown beyond what people think of me? Am I 100 percent honest and open all the time? I think not. I have to admit there are times when I still feel a twinge of thinking people won't like me when they really know me, or I will turn someone off if I say this or that. For me, I have to accept and be happy with progress, not perfection. I know I've come a long way since then. I intend to continue on the path to

Be Beautiful
Be Myself

and I hope you will, too!

Mandy Hale suggests that we be honest about who we are, flaws and all. She says we never know whom we will be inspiring by simply being ourselves.

This Week's Practice

Take time this week to stop and look deeply at the following questions:

Do I tell myself the truth?

Are there things about me I hide from myself or others?

If the answer is yes, what am I afraid of?

Write down your answers. It helps to journal here.

Prayer helps here. Praying for the courage to be who we are motivates us and helps to set an intention for us to move in that direction.

Then choose one thing you are afraid to tell someone and do this with a trusted friend. You will be amazed at how freeing this can be!

With God's help, I am gaining the
courage to be completely myself, wherever
I am and whomever I am with.

Time for Understanding

"Everything that irritates us about others can lead
us to an understanding of ourselves."

—*Carl Jung*

While watching *60 Minutes* one evening I learned quite
a lesson. When I saw the horrible things that were
done to Christians by ISIS I felt very angry. When a father
spoke of how ISIS wanted to take his ten-year-old daughter
so she could marry one of their men, a word I won't print
came up for me. I know that people are who they are because
of causes and conditions. I was still very angry!

In an attempt to calm myself down, I thought about some of the quotes on peace I had saved over the years:

> "The hardest people to forgive are enemies."
>
> —*Unknown Sage*

> "Our enemies are our greatest teachers."
>
> —*Unknown Sage*

> "Every being is an abode of God, worthy of respect and reverence."
>
> —*Hindu Scripture*

> "Understanding is the first step to acceptance, and only with acceptance can there be recovery."
>
> —*J. K. Rowling*

> "To 'love our enemy' is impossible because the moment we love him, he is no longer our enemy."
>
> —*Thich Nhat Hanh*

> "Be kind to unkind people. They need it the most."
>
> —*Unknown Sage*

All this helped me to remember to breathe, let myself feel my feelings, accept them, and still be gentle with myself.

In an attempt to understand people like ISIS I found a new word I didn't know the meaning of: *xenophobia*, pronounced zenə'fōbēə. It is defined as the unreasoned fear of that which is perceived to be foreign or strange; an intense or irrational dislike or fear of people from other countries.

People who belong to ISIS and other groups like them often learn at an early age to hate those who are different. They recruit and train others to think like they do. Their goal is to destroy those they think are their enemies. In a program at San Quentin State Prison, two inmates had the following insight, which makes a lot of sense: "Hurt people hurt people; healed people heal people."

The Boston Marathon bombing is another strong example of how hating those who are different can result in tragedy. As I am writing, the results of the trial have just been announced on television. The verdict is the death penalty for the bomber. My first reaction was "good!" He deserves it after killing so many innocent people and hurting so many more. Yes! This will make others think twice before they dare to harm others in our country.

I don't believe in the death penalty and I was surprised at my strong reaction. But it was just that—a reaction. Soon I settled down and knew that I don't believe in killing in any way. A verdict of life imprisonment in a federal prison is enough punishment, actually harder to envision than to be painlessly put to sleep.

Is there anything we can do about bombings, wars, and torture? Many think not. It has been going on since the beginning of civilization. Yet many think yes. There are certainly times when punishment is necessary.

The Dalai Lama teaches us, "Only the development of compassion and understanding for others can bring us the tranquility and happiness we all seek." If we don't see peace in our own lifetime, at least we will feel good as we fill our hearts with understanding, love, and purpose, and not fear and hate.

This Week's Practice

Practice being open this week to people who irritate you, make you angry, disappoint you, threaten you or others, that you are afraid of, hurt others, or that you don't like for any reason.

Be mindful of the feelings that come up for you when you see, think of, or read about this person or group. How do you feel? Are you angry, critical, fearful, irritated? Ask yourself the revealing question: *Is this how I want to feel?* If the answer is no, spend some time in an attempt to understand that person or group and where they are coming from. This isn't always easy or even possible. What we can know about people like those belonging to ISIS and other militant groups, is that they have been brainwashed from usually a very early age to think that they are doing what their God wants them to do. And they are promised they will be rewarded in heaven.

Knowing this does not mean we accept them but we can come closer to understanding them.

In the case of a next-door neighbor, a classmate, a friend or even a partner, we know that they haven't had the exact same upbringing, education, background, and experiences as we've had. They are who they are, as the Buddha teaches, because of their own causes and conditions.

This does not mean we accept unacceptable behavior. We can ask ourselves if there is an action step we can take to make the situation better. We can walk away from a person that causes suffering. We can look back at the practice week of Time for Releasing where we learned about the lesson of the God bag, box, or can. We learned to write down our feelings about the person, group, or situation, and put it in. This is a wonderful way to let it go. Every time it comes back up for you, know that you have turned it over. There is tremendous relief in this.

- Take time this week to be aware of those groups, countries, religions, philosophies, or persons you look down on, dislike, hate, or fear.
- Look deeply to see where these feelings came from. Have you formed these thoughts from your own experience, or have you been influenced by your parents, friends, teachers, books, or society?

- Think about what you can do to open your heart and your mind to have a greater understanding. This in no way means accepting destructive actions, but opening to understanding of why people may commit them.

I was deeply moved by Tim Hamm's song, "The Metta Song."[1] The lyrics say:

> . . . *May you be well, may you be happy, may you be peaceful and at ease.*
> *May you have courage, determination,*
> *And understanding for all you meet.*
> *May you be well . . . And for all living beings, especially my enemies,*
> *May we all be healthy and strong, and may we live in harmony.*

Let this be our practice for this week.

> *God is helping me to be open to*
> *understanding all people, regardless of*
> *their views and opinions, likes and dislikes,*
> *actions and non-actions. I am praying for*
> *understanding and open-heartedness,*
> *and that we may all live together*
> *in harmony and peace.*

---

1 http://timhammmusic.com/track/622797/the-metta-song?trackship_id=674686]

Time for Friendship

"We'll be friends forever, won't we, Pooh?"
asked Piglet.
"Even longer," Pooh answered.

—*A.A. Milne, Winnie-the-Pooh*

Without friends, I think life would be very lonely. I once read that we can call ourselves very lucky if we have two close friends in our lives. This is the kind of friend that doesn't judge us, the person we can say anything to and we know it is safe. This is the friend we can call any time day or night when we are troubled, or to share something good that has happened in our lives. This is the friend that, when they call us with the need to talk, we will drop almost anything to give them the time that they need. Sometimes we meet people and we just connect in a way that it feels as if we have known them our whole life. Other times a deep friendship can grow over the years.

Studies show the emotional support we get from friends and loved ones has a positive effect on our immune, hormonal, and cardiovascular systems, can lower blood pressure and cholesterol, and ultimately helps us live longer. Research also tells us that some of the values of having strong, meaningful relationships are that we have less susceptibility to disease; have an increased survival rate from heart attack; live a longer, healthier life; wake up with more hopefulness and a positive outlook; have increased vitality and zest; and life has greater meaning, purpose, and richness. Not to leave out the reason we do have friends in the first place: we like being with them and they make us feel good! These are a lot of reasons to make us nurture our friendships!

My friend, author, family therapist, and speaker, Sharon Wegscheider-Cruse, shares some wonderful thoughts on friendship. She writes, "We all need our friends. We need them for the good times and the bad. By connecting with friends, we feel comfort, connection, and safety. There are many connections we can call friends. Friends make us laugh, connect with our day-to-day life, and bring us new ideas and learning."

She describes the different kinds of friends. There are casual relationships. There are new friends. We might have friends that may have been in our life since childhood. We might have close friends, the ones we communicate with freely, trusting that all communication is between the two of us only and where there is a free flow of emotional energy. Sharon's friend Claudia Black says, "Surround yourself with people who respect you and treat you well."

This Week's Practice

Sharon tells us that keeping friendships alive is easier than ever. Modern technology is helping to make that happen. She writes, "Staying involved with their life as well as sharing our lives is so important. Write just one letter, write just one email, make one phone call each week to keep just one special friendship in your heart. The rewards will be great."

Once a week we can get together for coffee or lunch with a friend. We can put out a newsletter once a month. We can have a friend over for a meal. Do something with friends. Go to a movie, the beach, play cards or do anything else you enjoy together.

*I am so grateful for the friends I have
in my life today. No matter how busy I might be,
I am taking time to connect with at least
one friend this week. Keeping friendships alive is
such an important part of my happiness.*

Time for Congratulations!

The mountains and hills will break out
in song before you, and all the trees of the
countryside shall clap their hands.

—*The Bible, Book of Isaiah, 55:12*

This week will complete one full year of taking time for *you*! If you have been at all serious and practiced even a portion of the weeks, I am sure you have grown and feel better about yourself. Of course you can always go back and review and practice the weeks as often as you wish; spiritual growth is a lifetime practice, after all. As the saying goes, it's about progress, not perfection.

Take some time this week to review some of the pages to see if you have incorporated new habits into your life. While they are all important, here are some that I think are imperative if you are going to change and have a life filled with joy, peace, and purpose.

Meditation: Do you have a morning sitting practice?

Mindfulness: Are you practicing being more mindful throughout the day?

Gratitude: Do you daily think of at least one thing for which you are grateful?

Self-compassion: As you discover things about yourself that you might not like, do you treat yourself gently with love and compassion, and without judgment?

Purpose: Do you have a purpose each day?

Intention: Do you make an intention for each day before or after you meditate?

Fun: Do you take time for fun each day?

Acceptance: Are you learning to accept yourself and others without judgment?

Journaling: Have you incorporated a daily practice?

Forgiveness: Do you forgive as quickly as you can?

You might want to add other topics and make a daily or weekly checklist to keep track of your progress. And be sure you take time to congratulate yourself on your progress!

Dear Reader,

Here are six extra weeks. You might not have a need to spend a week on one particular subject in the first fifty-two weeks. Or you might see something in this section you would prefer to practice. Or you might even want to choose your own fifty-two weeks. Or you might even want to practice them all!

yes
i
did.

Time for "Did"

> "... a big part of intelligence is confidence and happiness, so boost both by pausing to list not the things you have yet to do, but rather all the things you've already accomplished."
>
> —*Amy Schumer*

A dear friend posted an interesting article on Facebook that was written by Amy Schumer in *Time* magazine (July 25, 2014). Amy suggested a "done list." This idea reminded me of the time, years ago, when I did beat myself up for all the things I didn't finish on my to-do list. Then one day it occurred to me that I had actually done ten out of twenty things and the realization felt good! Just shifting the focus on what we have accomplished rather than what we didn't get done lifts our spirits and makes those new neuron connections in our brains, which leads to our being happier, rather than beating ourselves up, which leads to our suffering.

Focusing on our to-do list can also lead to stress and anxiety. I know when I let myself think of everything I need to do I revert back to the old negative self-talk: "I'll never have enough time! I have too much to do!" In this state I get very little done. Or I'm full of anxiety. Or I'm not my best at what I am doing. Looking at the list to see what the most important thing is that we should do is the first step. Doing it and then acknowledging that it is done gives us the energy and confidence to go to the next item on our list.

Another advantage of focusing on our "done" list is that we are more open to doing our to-do list! My friend June wrote, "It took me a long time to realize that everything will get done eventually! I also found I must wait until the spirit moves me, and then a burst of energy comes over me, and it seems like, with little effort, it all gets done joyfully!"

Remember, when we shift our thoughts to something positive, our feel-good chemicals are triggered in our brain and our mood immediately shifts to feeling good.

This Week's Practice

This is an easy week. No hard work. No soul searching. Simply begin each day with a positive intention. You can say:

"Everything is flowing easily and effortlessly." (A quote I read many years ago by Shakti Gawain.) God gives me all the time and energy I need to do God's work.

You can use the ideas from the Time for Morning week: the wonderful morning practice of smiling upon awakening. It immediately prevents tension and worry from creeping in. Then expect something good to happen to you today. When the day goes by, focus on the things that are done!

It feels so good to be proud and grateful
for what I have done!

Time for Unblocking

"Freedom begins between the ears."

—*Edward Abbey*

Obsessive thinking keeps us from being in the present moment. The more we practice mindfulness, the more we will be aware of our obsessive thoughts and how they block us from being happy. Have you noticed that when you are worried about something, say a financial problem or a concern about a child or partner, that thought keeps repeating and repeating until you do something about it? It is said that worrying is like sitting in a rocking chair. You stay very busy but go nowhere.

Remember how neuroplasticity works (described earlier in the book). Each time we repeat a thought it makes deeper grooves in our brains. Then these thoughts become automatically triggered as soon as we hear, see, or think anything like it. For example, when my partner and I were beginning Serenity, Inc., our halfway house for alcoholic women, I would wake up with, *Where is the money for food coming from? How are we going to feed these women? How are we going to pay our bills?* I would repeat these thoughts over and over again until I learned about mindfulness and practiced saying to myself, *Breathing in peace, breathing out tension,* until my mind quieted down and I fell back asleep. By repeating these words, new grooves were formed in my brain while the old grooves faded, thus the old thoughts were no longer being triggered.

This Week's Practice

Tara Brach has a wonderful exercise to help stop obsessive thinking. She suggests we keep a journal of all our obsessive thoughts for a few days. Choose two or three that keep us stuck in shame, anger, fear, anxiety, etc., and find a simple name or label for it such as financial worries. She strongly suggests that we notice them with acceptance and friendliness, not judgment and say, "Real but not true." We let ourselves feel the feeling resulting from the thought. Then we acknowledge that the feeling is real but the thought isn't real.

The wonderful part of this is we are not denying the thought is real. Yes, our minds thought the thought and then our bodies felt the feeling triggered by the thought. But when we label it and return to those great questions from Byron Katie and Thich Nhat Hanh, "Is it true?" and "Are you sure?" We have a new perspective. We have the ability to question the validity of our obsessive thinking, replacing the old grooves with new, more positive ones.

Another very simple step in stopping obsessive thinking is breathing. As we develop the regular habit of mindfulness, we become aware of our obsessive thoughts more quickly. As soon as you notice one, *stop*, and be aware as you *breathe* in and out three times. You'll find by the third breath the worrying thought will have disappeared.

It is so freeing to know I do not have
to believe all my thoughts!

Time for Realism

"Shoot for the moon. Even if you miss,
you'll land among the stars."

—*Les Brown*

As a child I loved sports. At summer camp I was the second best in *all* sports. And I was happy! I didn't want to concentrate on one sport and be the best in it. I didn't want to give up all the other sports just to be the best in one. I accepted my second-best status.

Then over the years I read many books and emails telling me that I can be anything I want to be. Maybe I could have been best in all sports after all! Maybe I can be better than who I am now! All I have to do is what they were telling me to do. There was a time I believed it. Maybe if I did what they are suggesting, if I tried harder, if I took more courses, I would make more money, sell more books, and on and on.

People might write that we can be anything we want to be, but can we be better than who we are? Can we be better than our ability? How many presidents of the United States can there be at the same time? How many pitchers for Major League Baseball teams can there be? How many women can win an Academy Award for best actress each year? How many people can win the race?

Obviously, if we aspire to be any of these and just don't have the ability, we are going to be miserable all our lives. We are going to feel like failures. This is why, when I wrote my book on affirmations, *Change Almost Anything in 21 Days*, I included the word *almost*. We can't change everything!

How do we know when we have reached our best? What if we have reached our limit for now? Every time I had these questions, these lines from the poem Desiderata, by Max Ehrmann helped me:

"If you compare yourself with others, you may become vain or bitter, for always there will be greater and lesser persons than yourself."

I find a great deal of peace in this.

Once we come to the place where we know we are doing our best and can accept who we are, we can be happy. This doesn't mean we stop training or stop trying to be better tomorrow. It simply means doing our best each day, so we can end our day knowing we have done our best.

This Week's Practice

Spend some time this week meditating and journaling on these questions:

Do I do my best?

Is there realistically more I could do next time?

Am I being honest with myself?

Can I be satisfied with where I am in my life today?

If not, what can I do to say yes to that question?

It feels so good to know that
I am doing my best and I am exactly
where I am supposed to be
in this moment.

Time for RAIN

"It helps to remember that our spiritual practice is not about accomplishing anything— not about winning or losing—but about ceasing to struggle and relaxing as it is."

—*Pema Chödrön*

While of course there is always time for rain and sunshine, this is a different kind of RAIN. Here, RAIN is an acronym, which is an abbreviation formed from the first letters of a phrase. The acronym RAIN was first coined by Michele McDonald. It has been found in Tara Brach's book *Radical Acceptance* and Jack Kornfeld has said it. When we follow these four steps we can change our negative habits, which create suffering, and replace them with new and positive habits which bring us happiness. RAIN helps to understand our unconscious patterns. So when you are feeling uncomfortable in any way, practice RAIN.

R stands for Recognize what is happening. See your thoughts, emotions, feelings, and sensations. Recognize what is happening inside of you right now.

A stands for Accept it. Accept whatever is happening in this moment. Don't push it away by shutting down or looking for something to eat or drink or smoke. Accept it. Be gentle. You might want to say to yourself, *This is okay. Easy does it.*

I stands for Investigate. Investigate your inner experience with kindness. Be gentle again. Be curious. Is it pleasant, unpleasant, or neutral? What emotions does it bring up in you? Do you tell yourself stories about how you feel or blame it on someone or something?

N stands for Non-personal, Non-attachment—resting in Natural awareness. Author and meditation teacher Tara Brach writes in her book *True Refuge* that when our identification with our ego becomes loosened, we begin to love from openness and love.

This Week's Practice

Take some time this week to practice RAIN each day. You'll find it is a wonderful addition to your life, once you form the habit.

It feels so good to know I get let go of thoughts and feel peace by accepting each moment as it is.

Time for No-Thought

How do we get to a place where there is no thought, when we are completely and always at peace in the moment, no matter what is going on? Fortunately my teachers over the years have assured me that life is far busier than in the days of the Buddha, when the monks' only concerns were to be mindful, to beg for food, listen to teachings, and walk, eat, and sleep. Perhaps we can get there by doing a three-month silent retreat, or living alone in a cave for a year or more. Some have. But, most likely, with our busy, responsible lives, our minds will become gradually quieter with practice, and we will have to settle for more and more *moments* of peace, of no-thought.

Zen Master Thich Nhat Hanh writes, "When we offer ourselves deeper silence of not thinking, when we find that space and calm inside, then without effort we radiate peace and joy. We are able to help others and create a healing environment around us, without uttering a single word." He has a wonderful way of referring to our busy minds. In his book *Silence: The Power of Quiet in a World Full of Noise*, he writes that there's a radio playing in our head, Radio Station NST (Non-Stop Thinking). "Our mind is filled with noise, and that's why we can't hear the call of life, the call of love. Our heart is calling us, but we don't hear. We don't have time to listen to our heart."

Mindfulness quiets the noise inside us. Without mindfulness we can be lost in regret and sorrow about the past or filled with fear and worry about the future. We just have to follow our in-breath and our out-breath, making space for silence. We say to ourselves: *Breathing in, I know I'm breathing in. Breathing out, I know I'm breathing out.* Please note that *no thought* is not the same as *thoughtless*. No thought is that peaceful space, the gap that occurs in between breaths. It happens when we are one with the moment in deep listening and deep concentration. Thoughtless, on the other hand, is that selfish time filled with our own ego, when we are only thinking of ourselves at the expense of someone else.

This Week's Practice

This week, in your morning meditation, take five minutes or so to say: "Breathing in, I know I'm breathing in. Breathing out, I know I'm breathing out."

During the day stop for a few moments and bring your awareness to your breath, repeating the same phrase. The more often you do this, the more often you will be creating new pathways in your brain. You are forming a new habit that will eventually become automatic.

Meditation teacher Bill Menza wrote, "Another way to stop your mind from doing a lot of thinking is to focus on a place in your body. This could be at your nostrils and lungs as you breathe in and breathe out. Or it could be the center of your body which is an inch or two below your navel. Keep your mind there for as long as possible as you simultaneously follow your breathing. Do this 100 percent. Notice anything different?"

When you find yourself in the past or the future, saying *stop* or *shhhh* works. Follow this with three breaths in and out.

Remember the practice of wearing a rubber band around your wrist in an earlier week? This works very well in helping you remember that there is something for you to remember!

It feels so good to know I can stop anytime
I feel stressed, fearful or angry, breathe,
and empty my mind.

Time for Enlightenment

> Before enlightenment—chop wood,
> carry water. After enlightenment—
> chop wood, carry water."
>
> —*Zen Buddhist Proverb*

The word *enlightenment* holds so much promise for us. Eckhart Tolle defines enlightenment as rising above our thoughts. In Buddhism it means awakening and understanding, someone who is no longer imprisoned by their cravings. The word *Buddha* means "the awakened one."

Another way to look at the word enlightenment is to focus on the *lighten* part of it. We lighten our load. We become lighter when we give up our cravings, desires, addictions, and longings.

Imagine you have been on a path to enlightenment this year. On one side is anger and greed and fear, all things leading to suffering. On the other side is gratitude, generosity, compassion, empathy, and forgiveness, all things that lead us to joy, happiness, and freedom. Of course we say we would choose the side with gratitude. But do we really? We still sometimes have fear and anger. We still want for ourselves above others. We still suffer.

Thich Nhat Hanh has a wonderful image that is very helpful for this. He teaches us that we have a store consciousness within us. Here lies all of the characteristics there are: anger, fear, hatred, joy, generosity, faith, and so on. Imagine they are like seeds and it is up to us what we choose to water. If we water the seeds that bring us suffering, which he calls weeds, we will suffer. If we water the seeds that bring us joy, joy is what we will feel. As we water the positive seeds, they get larger while the negative seeds, the seeds that bring us suffering stop growing. We become lighter, more peaceful, more joyful.

Spiritually speaking, enlightenment and awakening can be the same. In Alcoholics Anonymous, the twelve steps are taught as a way of life. Again we let go of our cravings, our addiction. We turn to a power greater than ourselves. We let go our negative, destructive habits, our resentments, our character defects. We make amends. We pray and meditate, bringing us closer to the God of our understanding. The Twelve Steps promise us that we will no longer regret the past or fear the future. The last step, the Twelfth Step, promises us a spiritual awakening "as a result of practicing these steps." We become "awake" in the present moment.

Enlightenment can also be a shift in one's consciousness. We can become enlightened and awake when we practice the "time fors" in this book. We become happier, better people. We find joy and purpose in our lives. It's no longer all about us, our egos, but rather, it's more about our interconnectedness. We become more compassionate, loving, and generous. We have a higher calling, a desire to help others, to end their suffering, to help to bring peace to our precious, hurting world. It is a time for peace, a time for joy.

This last week does not have to be the end but a continuation, a way of life. We can go back to any week and spend more time with the ones that need more practice. We can move forward and take some time with the extra weeks. *Time for Me* is a way of life.

This Week's Practice

Spend some time looking back and seeing the progress you have made with each week. Mark a star at the weeks you feel you have completed. Put a question mark at the weeks you think might need more time.

It would be good to make a commitment and set an intention to continue the suggestions that were most helpful in your life. I hope you have made these action steps a part of your life:

Morning meditation

Setting your intention for the day each morning

Developing a practice of bringing mindfulness to your twenty-four hours

Looking for ways to help others

Developing a daily gratitude list

Always taking some time for you

Add whatever else you think is important to this list. Then congratulate yourself for your progress! Even if you have accomplished only a few weeks to your satisfaction, you're ahead of where you were a year ago.

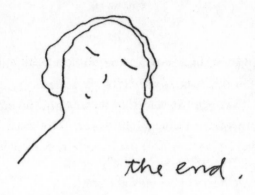

the end.

In Closing

Dear Readers,

Sometimes I worry about sounding too positive, too unrealistic.

Sometimes I worry I am sounding too preachy, as if I know what is right for you and you should listen to me. What I have really tried to do in *Time for Me* and my other books is pass on what teachers have told me, messages that have inspired me, and experiences I have had that have helped me to suffer less and find more joy, peace, compassion, purpose, and love in my life.

My goal is a simple one: to do what I can to help us all to expand our awareness, so that we can reduce our own suffering, help others reduce their suffering, and thus reduce the suffering in the world. If people suffer less, they will be happy. They will hate less, they will blame less, and they will leave others alone who are different.

We have a choice each and every day.

We can begin by *taking time for me*.

We can practice what we find in this book one week at a time.

We can begin our day with meditation and prayer.

We can ask for God's will for us and ask for the power to carry that out.

We can make an intention to be the best person we can be, to be mindful as we go through the day, conscious of how we can help others and be kind to ourselves and others.

If we do these simple things each day we will be happier and more peaceful, and we will be making a difference in the world, one person at a time.

Thank you for joining me, one day at a time. I am blessed to have you all in my life. I hope you know that together we are making a difference.